THE ART OF LIVING

THE ART

Nadine Crenshaw

# of Living

Simple Wisdom for the Self

Prima Publishing

For the childhood sweetheart who turned out to be
the love of my life,
and my greatest teacher as well,
Robert Crenshaw

Interior Design by Trina Stahl

Library of Congress Cataloging-in-Publication Data
Crenshaw, Nadine.
The art of living : simple wisdom for the self / Nadine Crenshaw.
p. cm.
ISBN 0-7615-1236-5
1. Conduct of life. I. Title.
BJ1581.2.C74 1998
170'.44—dc21 97-53265
CIP

98 99 00 01 02 HH 10 9 8 7 6 5 4 3 2 1
Printed in the United States of America

I quote others only the better to express myself.

MONTAIGNE

CONTENTS

INTRODUCTION
An Overview of the Art of Living

> *Living on Earth has always been a dangerous way to spend your time.* ANNE LAMOTT

Something disastrous has happened. Despite the hundreds of electronic devices that protect and serve us and increase our expectations, our lives are becoming more tedious and less significant. To alleviate our inner boredom, we invent extravagant outer lives, filling our free hours with play that is hardly distinguishable from work. Our inner selves, meanwhile, shrivel. To recover a sense of vitality we give vent to ever more primitive and unconscious elements. Why else would we willingly watch movies and read books full of such infamies as are popular today?

Meanwhile, our mechanical routines result in a forfeiture of self-esteem that few primitive societies would condone. To bear it, we function on autopilot, more asleep than awake. We're learning the unpleasant truth that, despite computers and jet planes, a satisfying life is not guaranteed. No software yet designed can program us to live well—because life always has and always will function from the inside out. It's time we filter out the extraneous noise and listen to our inner voices, because the things we feel inside, about ourselves and about our lives, are what life mirrors back at us.

That mirroring makes for some difficulties. It means that

each of us must figure out how to live well inside our own skins. That entails simplifying and bringing everything into better balance. How do we do that? What are the best ways to approach life? Is there some secret "art of living," and do we each have to discover it for ourselves—must we reinvent the wheel?

In some respects, yes, and that has its thrilling aspects: to participate in the co-creation of our own lives and the world we want to live in is an exciting challenge. It's also frightening. But help is available. People throughout history have noted their own progress in learning the art of living, and much of that wisdom has been preserved. This information has never been concealed, but it has been ignored.

In fact, most "new" ideas about satisfying our spirits' deepest longings aren't new at all. They are only past ideas rediscovered and rephrased by modern minds.

Knowledge comes, but wisdom lingers.

ANONYMOUS

This book is an attempt to put the age-old wisdom into a contemporary context. It does not pretend to be a complete compendium of wisdom, but it may serve as a starting point. The quotes in *The Art of Living* are taken from a broad range of sources, some old, some new. We shouldn't dismiss ideas as unimportant simply because they seem like common sense, or because they offer advice we've heard a hundred times before. Sayings become worn because the meaning behind them is so useful. The remarkable thing is that the wisdom of our ancestors and of our contemporaries is so in agreement.

This is meant to be a personal book, but not all the ideas will be beneficial to everyone. Each of us must pick and choose the ideas which are relevant to our circumstances. The format of *The Art of Living* broadly follows the most common stages we must unravel on our road from adulthood to old age. We begin, as children do, inside ourselves. We learn why *now*—this moment—is the only moment of life any of us truly has, and how contemplation can help us see that now is enough. Also, we discuss the most vital factor of the art of living: valuing ourselves.

In "Putting Ourselves First," we learn how the simple expedient of choosing to be cheerful can change everything. And we see how the self-confident person asserts herself.

> ***When you have means but are not getting anywhere, seek appropriate associates, and you will be lucky.***
>
> *I CHING*

Once we are whole within ourselves, and know how to move about in the world without losing that wholeness, we consider "Sharing Ourselves" with others. Everyone needs good friendships. Of course, we hope to find love, too, and we want to know how to coax its first tender leaves into vigorous growth. If love and desire combine strongly enough, the natural thing is to marry. Marriage is possibly the most profound sharing of ourselves, involving fusion with another.

Marriage usually leads to "Creating a Family." It's good to know why we have such a strong urge to beget new generations so that we can explore our personal desires in this regard. Parenthood, like it or not, is a new stage of growth—for parents as well as children. And living with teenagers is easier if we understand how to appeal to the human idealism that is at its peak in teens.

As we go on to "Life's Work," we discuss ambition and how to harness it to reach our goals. We also grapple with definitions of success.

In "Life After Work," we see that too much of anything is unsettling. There are times when having it all feels like being caught in an avalanche. We'll address the value of seeking balance in our lives. In order to do so, we need to know the difference between money and prosperity.

> ***Measure wealth not by the things you have, but by the things you have for which you would not take money.***
> ANONYMOUS

Sometimes unwanted change is thrust on us. "When We Must Start Over" deals with the shock of disaster—losing loved ones or losing our self-identity, such as through a job loss or a handicapping injury. We don't have to rub our hands together, answerless, when dealing with life-warping events. We can instead reinvent ourselves.

As the years pass, we find ourselves "Bearing Up Against Time." When we wake up to find we've become middle-aged, the realization is doubly dismaying if we also discover that our parents now need our help.

> ***If there is a sin against life, it consists perhaps not so much in despairing of life as in hoping for another life and in eluding the implacable grandeur of this life.***
> ALBERT CAMUS

To some, retirement means a narrowing down of life. "The Ebb Tide" discusses using our retirement years to expand our lives, to seek an attitude of agelessness as we continue to eat from the buffet of life. Which doesn't mean that we can be blind to the fact that death is suddenly as close as our own shadows. It has always been that close, however, and it stands behind everyone, whether one day old or one hundred years old. We'll explore how it can be faced with dignity.

Though many will read straight through *The Art of Living,* the book is arranged so that readers can turn to any stage of life. But just reading about wisdom handed down from generation to generation is not enough to make us wise ourselves. We have to incorporate that wisdom into our lives. To that end, we should think about the discussions and the quotes, let the ideas resonate in our minds and spirits, play with them and debate them. To make ideas personally meaningful, use the affirmations and the sections titled "To Think and Write About."

Some may doubt the benefits of affirmations. But shouldn't we be willing to employ every possible technique to give ourselves the best possible chances of success? To affirm ourselves is equivalent to stepping up to the starting mark with a strong intention to win. An affirmation declares positively and formally that we are equal to the challenge (or willing to *grow* equal to it) and that we are heading in a particular direction.

To affirm means to "make firm" in our minds. Affirmations can help us do difficult things, acknowledge profound obstacles, or perform better than we have previously. If the wording of the affirmations given in *The Art of Living* does not strike echoes within us, we certainly may construct our own wordings. There are an infinite number of ways to affirm a single thought, and each of us must find that one distinct and perhaps unexpected way that suits us best. However, there are three directives for forming affirmations: seek positive ways to express the statement, state it in the present tense, and keep it simple and memorable.

For those who take the suggestion of starting a journal, phrases that can be used as affirmations are likely to appear in our writing. (More about journal-keeping in a moment.)

Finally, affirmations need to be *used* if they are to be incorporated into the fabric of our being. By writing them ten times each and chanting them aloud, we hardwire them into our systems.

The "To Read and Think About" suggestions involve using a journal. Those who have never kept a journal may begin one now. Any ordinary spiral-bound notebook will do. The process is simple. Date entries, then record thoughts and ideas about the issues discussed in *The Art of Living.* For example, say we are interested in the issue of having a baby. So many considerations bob in our minds that we can get frustrated trying to sort them out. Sometimes just thinking about such a complex problem is confusing. It's rather like trying to play a game of chess in our head. We must try to remember where each piece is on the board, and at the same time figure how moves of various pieces will be responded to by the opposition. . . . It's too much! What a relief to have a real chess board and game pieces before us. Making decisions is likewise much easier when we can see everything at once. It is easier to have our thoughts about any complex issue right in front of our eyes. Written thoughts don't appear one minute and disappear the next. Suddenly, we can weigh the pros and cons calmly.

A journal is a real day-in and day-out utility tool for learning the art of living. Using the quotes and discussions provided here as jumping-off points, we can make real progress in finding our own answers to the questions of how to live well.

> ***We are much at the mercy of words. They govern our thoughts more often than they obey them.***
>
> J. MIDDLETON MURRY

Because much of what we write in our journals will be profoundly personal, we keep them private. A journal may be the only place where we have total freedom of expression. We can write whatever we like, in whatever manner we like, even if it's in a shorthand of twiddles, dots, and curlicues. If we can read it, that's all that matters, for we are the only ones who *should* read it.

The golden nuggets of self-discovered wisdom we capture can surprise us. And if some of those thoughts are less than golden, we shouldn't be concerned. A journal serves to record who we are right now. Unpleasant thoughts don't mean that we are unpleasant. They say that we *felt* unpleasant at the moment they were written. Days or even hours after making a journal entry, we can read what we have penned and see how much we've grown. Over time, a journal can serve as a history of our very personal growth.

A journal helps to chronicle memories, thc workings of our imaginations, feelings, dreams, intuitions, and creative urges. When we use a journal to bring our inner selves into an active relationship with our rational, practical minds, the mental fusion releases tremendous energy.

Given all these benefits, can any of us really afford to go on living *without* keeping a journal?

Do not take life too seriously, you will never get out of it alive. ELBERT HUBBARD

There is one other element in this book that warrants mention: humor. Some quotes in *The Art of Living* are there simply to remind us not to live too soberly, not to swallow our smiles, not to let a day pass without laughter. Please read them in that light.

The Art of Living should be referred to over and over. Desired changes take time. At first, we naturally revert to old ways of thinking and behaving. As this happens, we should review the relevant passages in *The Art of Living* to remind us of the direction we want to take.

With luck, this book will become a reference that will support the fullest possible realizations of ourselves. If it gives even a little help in that direction, then it will have achieved its purpose.

> *Ideals are like stars; you will not succeed in touching them with your hands, but like the seafaring man on the desert of waters, you choose them as your guides, and following them, you reach your destiny.*
>
> CARL SCHURZ

Part One

The Inner Self

Chapter 1

Living in the Now

O Fair Today

Why thus longing, thus forever sighing
For the far-off, unattain'd, and dim,
While the beautiful all round thee lying
Offers up its low, perpetual hymn?

HARRIET SEWALL

The present moment is priceless, but sadly, few of us even notice it. Nor do we often meet people who really understand that it is priceless. They are rare, and they tend to live quietly, enjoying life, loving other people, loving the universe, behaving decently, wisely, charitably. Such people seem able to let go of guilt, fear, and negativity. They take careful stock of how they spend their energies. They may possess no singular powers or knowledge; their impact may be as soft as moonlight. They may not even be especially admired. Nor do they crave powers or knowledge or admiration.

On the other hand, most of us live lives that are regularly banal and often painful. We aren't even aware of how removed our lives are from the source of beauty and creativity. We try to experience true, deep, joyful, peace through drinking a martini and watching a sitcom. It doesn't work. We don't know about the present moment, or don't notice it, and so the most priceless gift of joy possible to us goes ignored. We're too busy striving for more money or more approval.

> ***Modern man lives increasingly in the future and neglects the present. A people who seek to do this have an insatiable demand for soothsayers and oracles to assure and comfort them about the insubstantial road they tread.***
>
> LOREN EISELEY

Foolishly, we defer enjoying our lives until we get to be more important, more secure, more adored than we are today. We hurt other people, and society, and our planet in order to find status and goods that promise the great happiness we've been awaiting. Failing to understand that the present moment is precious, we don't see the good things we have in our lives right *now.* We don't keep our senses open to the subtle pleasures of ordinary existence.

We worry about yesterday endlessly, while on the other hand, tomorrow tantalizes, like a night landscape lit with weird, inverted light. We can pick out this, and that . . . but we can't be sure. We can do nothing with the future but plan and hope for the best.

The Stress Reduction Clinic of the University of Massachusetts trains people to cultivate a greater calm, nonjudgmental, moment-to-moment awareness—what Buddhists call mindfulness. The clinic's program focuses completely on training mainstream Americans in awareness. It's one of many efforts to counteract our vast range of stress and pain. Awareness grounds us in the now. It places us between the too-certain past (which no longer exists) and the uncertain future (which doesn't yet exist). It puts us here, in this present moment, which holds all the rapture and magic of life at its quickening point.

> ***He remembered the rain, and the sleep, and the feel of beach sand beneath his feet, and the ocean rolling in to whisper its eternal song . . .***
>
> HARLAN ELLISON

Let's look at it from a practical stance: Our world is composed of only three time zones—yesterday, today, and tomorrow. Focusing our minds exclusively on yesterday or tomorrow gets us into difficulties and renders us ineffective today. The past is an information bank from which we can learn, but it is not a web in which we are caught. It is in the present moment alone that we can use our powers to move our lives forward—to decide, to do, to be, to control. Our only point of control is in the present—the now.

Choices about change, for instance, can only be made in the present. The first condition for fruitful change is to see clearly where we *are*. We can't hide from our present reality; it stays with us unless we are willing to change it *in the present moment*. For a simplistic example, consider Carmen, who bought a house with flooring the color of tobacco spit. For three years she told everyone she was going to do something about that flooring "soon." Not until she centered herself in the moment could she go shopping for a new floor covering. She stopped waiting for the future and did it now.

> ***Think about it. If you want to move the chair you're sitting on, you can only do it in the present. . . . You cannot move the chair in either the past or the future.*** CHARLES J. GIVENS

If there are aspects of the present we don't like, we can start to plan how to change them, but if we pretend those aspects don't exist, we will never change them.

Imagine someone in an *Indiana Jones* sort of predicament, needing to cross an abyss of lava. The only way to the other side is via a series of flat-topped pillars jutting above the inferno. As our friend starts across, moving from pillar to pillar, at any moment his only stability lies on the pillar directly under him. Let his attention wander and he dramatically increases the likelihood of getting fried. The point is that even in the worst scenario, gaining a steadfast foothold in life comes from accepting our present circumstances, no matter how much we might long to be elsewhere.

If yesterday is only a memory and tomorrow is only a dream, then now is all that is real.

The butterfly counts not months but moments, and has time enough.

RABINDRANATH TAGORE

Being poised above an abyss of lava would certainly make us notice—really notice!—our present moment. But what happens if we notice, say, right *now?*

Why, immediately all the minute points of our existence appear as if sharply lit. By unveiling our inner eyes, we find immense beauty hidden in the inconsequential details of everyday life. Clearing our inner ears, we hear the subtle, lovely harmony of the universe everywhere. Opening our hearts, we take pleasure in the people around us—family, friends, strangers, even those who are less than perfect, as we are less than perfect. Opening our inner selves to the beauty, the enigma, the grandeur of ordinary existence, we realize that it has always been beautiful, enigmatic, and grand, and will always be so.

> ***The world is a mirror of infinite beauty, yet no man sees it. It is a temple of majesty, yet no man regards it. It is a region of Light and Peace, did not men disquiet it. It is the Paradise of God.***
>
> THOMAS TRAHERNE

What does it take to achieve this opening of our senses and hearts? Some call it mindfulness, some call it consciousness, some call it awareness. It is a form of meditation, and can be a form of prayer. For many it is a foreign idea, "Oriental," and therefore somehow foreboding. The motivation to practice it is different for each person. Many people come to it out of a desire to know the Creator. Others in order to understand their own minds. In a world moving at hyperspeed, when so many of us are anxious, any move toward contemplating things deeply rooted and eternal, things that forever *are,* is desirable.

However, the practice of mindfulness is also worthwhile simply as a means of savoring our lives. The present moment is an always available quiet cove where the waters are still and lucid enough to see all the way to the inscrutable depths.

> ***Life is like an ice cream cone, you have to lick it one day at a time.*** CHARLES SCHULTZ

It is not difficult to find time for mindfulness, and it is worth the effort. Carving out the time will bring us a sense of wholeness. It does not take a special place, special clothing, or unique rituals. We can do it on a crowded streetcar as easily as all alone in a place of beauty. The basis of the practice is this: Simply participate directly in the moment in which we are now alive, with as much awareness and understanding as possible. Shut out the clamor of the expired past and the projected future, and become quiet.

> *The best preparation for the future, is the present well seen to . . .* GEORGE MACDONALD

We've all developed some degree of mindfulness already. Just to read a book, to live our complicated lives, takes a certain amount of awareness and concentration. Those qualities of mind are already available to us. They can be intensified through gentle perseverance. Without any undue strain on our schedules, we can set aside a little time every once in a while to experience inner silence and this precious moment, this transient little parenthesis in eternity.

We value the future and we value the past. Why don't we value *now?* This moment is tomorrow's past. Must it be lost to us before we honor it?

For a long time, a young woman called Dawn felt her life was just about ready to begin—her real life, that is. But there was always some obstacle in the way, college to be got through, some unfinished family business, then a favor to be paid back. Always, she thought that as soon as she could manage it, her life would begin. Finally, on her twenty-fifth birthday, a shock ran through her. She realized: "This *is* my life."

> *This is my life; I'm not going to have this moment again.* BERNIE SEIGEL

The person who lives in the future, waiting for just the right moment to begin her real life, will find her real life slipping by her. Every person's solemn duty is to live right here, right now.

Too many of us are hurrying through our lives, filled with

drive and ambition. We're eagerly gathering material rewards, slighting our integrity. But all our dashing around can't help us avoid that deep, unrecognized need to feel comfort. We contain the key to that comfort, and to completeness and health. It's in awareness.

I've shut the door on yesterday
And thrown the key away—
To-morrow holds no fears for me,
Since I have found to-day.

VIVIAN YEISER LARAMORE

Awareness is not a state most of us can maintain all the time. We get busy; then we notice that we're feeling separated from ourselves again, and from others, and from life itself. A sort of darkness falls on us, closing us off. But if for even short periods each day we can simply see—moment to moment—what's occurring, observing it without judgment or preference, then we can't get lost in the hurricane.

And as awareness more deeply centers us, we once in a while experience our true natural condition, our natural state of being, our inner self that is, like the sun, always shining, always present, though often obscured. We then perceive that we are blocked from our own natural light only by the clouds of our thoughts and longings and fears. We live in the overcast condition of trying to exist in three time zones at once, but we know we can return to the priceless present, and to ourselves, whenever we want.

Yesterday is something we no longer have. Tomorrow is something we may never have. When we don't get lost in moments that are gone or yet to come, we are left with this moment. What we have is the present.

Eternity is a terrible thought. I mean, where is it going to end? TOM STOPPARD

AFFIRMATION

I make time each day to give all my awareness to the very moment in which I am living, with all its sights and sounds and tastes.

TO THINK AND WRITE ABOUT

The fact that this book captured your attention says that you have started your journey, that you are willing to cultivate the elemental aspects of the art of living. But are you still reluctant to record your thoughts in a journal? It may make you feel more comfortable to realize that there is no "correct" or "best" way to keep a journal. You need not even use complete sentences. Lists, phrases, incomplete thoughts—all are fine.

Try this: Simply describe this moment—where you are, what you see, hear, smell, taste, feel *right now.*

There, you have just affirmed your own existence and validated your vision of the world during the moment you described. You have made your version of reality official.

Journal writing is a wonderful way of staying in touch with what is important to you and who you want to be.

Chapter 2

Valuing Ourselves

The Beginnings of a Lifelong Romance

Make peace with yourself, and heaven and earth will make peace with you. Endeavor to enter your own inner cell, and you will see the heavens; because the one and the other are one and the same, and when you enter one you see the two.

SAINT ISAAC OF SYRIA

Unless we value ourselves above everyone and everything else, we aren't ready to live well.

Is that a jarring thought?

Most of us are not prepared to learn the art of living, because we are handicapped by a dislike of ourselves. Simply in the course of growing up, we develop distinctly unfriendly feelings toward ourselves. The process is not the fault of bad parents or of living in a bad environment. *Everybody* collects bad self-feelings. We get them from the media, which asks us ceaselessly to compare ourselves to picture-perfect, fictional people and situations. We get them from our own mistakes, which we don't know how to forgive. And we get them from acquaintances out to make themselves feel better at our expense. We are human flypaper, picking up whichever self-unfriendly opinions happen to buzz near us.

Coming into adulthood, we are handicapped indeed, though it may not show as plainly as the loss of an arm or a leg. We have no idea what it feels like to take pride in an accomplishment. Sadly, many, if not most, of us spend our whole lives in this state. Looking around, everyone else seems to radiate a sense of self-worth. We alone feel haunted by feeling that we aren't good enough, by a sense of low self-worth. This belief causes us misery.

> ***The mind is its own place, and in itself***
> ***Can make a Heav'n of Hell, a Hell of Heav'n.***
>
> JOHN MILTON

Whether we call this self-unfriendliness "negative self-talk," "self-sabotaging behavior," "lack of self-confidence," "low self-esteem," or even "psychic masochism," it all boils down to the same thing—an unloving, even hostile attitude toward our very selves.

When we don't feel friendly toward ourselves, it makes no difference what we achieve, what happiness we cause others, what education we absorb—we cannot feel satisfied. If we don't value ourselves independently of our achievements, we will not even value our achievements!

Most of us are sensitive, thoughtful people, yet we see the flaws in our natures as big and bright as neon billboards, proclaiming our unworthiness in letters too large to be ignored. The result is that we don't feel okay, at least not in any persistent or abiding way. Those of us who struggle to live well despite such a disadvantage are truly courageous—but of course we'd never think to give ourselves that much credit.

It is the mind that maketh good or ill,
That maketh wretch or happy, rich or poor.

EDMUND SPENSER

How can we change this fact? The single most important step is to begin to address ourselves in a positive manner. The best way for us to grow more self-friendly is simply to speak to ourselves tenderly and encouragingly—or, if that is too much to ask, at least speak to ourselves with the courtesy we would give a stranger.

After a lifetime of self-contempt, this may be harder than it sounds. It requires accepting the fact that our personal, unique value does not depend on our origins or our talents any more than it depends on what we do. We must try to hold on to an attitude of what Carl Rogers called "unconditional personal regard."

All of you reading these words have loved someone, have done someone a kindness, have healed a wound, have taken on a challenge, have created something beautiful, and have enjoyed breathing the air of existence. Never doubt how precious, how vitally important you are. Every moment you make a difference. *RANDOM ACTS OF KINDNESS*

This notion of loving ourselves is age-old. "You can't love anyone else unless you love yourself first." How many times have we heard that? It's a cliché. It's trite, hackneyed, corny. Right? But remember, clichés get to be clichés by being *used* so often. Improving any area in our lives begins with modifying our self-image. Our thoughts about ourselves define our outer lives. They affect how we respond to our experiences. Valuing ourselves helps us build our lives on a secure foundation. It also helps us become our own helper, adviser, friend, and therapist.

Conversely, if we undervalue ourselves, we almost certainly are applying double standards: We're underrating ourselves just because we're us and not someone else. We may be disappointed in ourselves because we haven't come up to an exclusive set of personal standards, and we're whipping ourselves for it mercilessly.

Man is what he believes. ANTON CHEKHOV

Confidence, love, inner strength, joy, ecstasy—these are empowering states that depend upon a wellspring of self-love. In its absence, there can only be self-hate, which supplies the paralyzing states of confusion, depression, fear, anxiety, sadness, frustration, and powerlessness. When we don't love ourselves, we cannot possibly sustain a response to the world in which we're excited, sure of success, crackling with energy, and mentally alive. Without self-love, we can't be as useful to the world as our potential promises.

Confidence? Respect? We produce these states within ourselves. How we picture ourselves in our minds, and what and how we speak to ourselves, is reflected in our behavior—in what we say, do, and *are* in the world. What we think about ourselves even affects our physiology—our posture, our biochemistry, our level of energy, our very breathing.

The ancestor of every action is a thought.

RALPH WALDO EMERSON

When we believe that something is true, we literally live in the state of its being true. Therefore, belief in ourselves helps us tap the richest resources deep within us, creating and directing these resources to the support of our desired outcomes. It is our belief in ourselves that determines how much of our potential we'll be able to tap.

If there is a faith that can move mountains, it is faith in your own power.

MARIE VON EBNER ESCHENBACH

People who love themselves feel autonomous. What does that mean? It means they're not overly preoccupied by the hurts or injustices they receive. They don't feel injured when the boss doesn't appreciate their work; they don't run themselves down for making a mistake; they don't let Uncle Joe make them feel stupid.

You are, we all are, the culmination of an infinite number of improbable gifts from myriad nameless sources. DAWNA MARKOVA

It's passive to let others define us. If we have a slave mentality, we will be slaves. We always have to be our own best friends. That doesn't mean we spoil ourselves; it doesn't mean we don't ever do things we don't want to do. It means that we do things we don't want to do because *in the end* they will benefit us.

Sounds terribly selfish, doesn't it? Well, this kind of selfishness is absolutely necessary. (Here's an undiscussed truth: People who are extremely generous are that way not out of selflessness—just the opposite. They get a great deal out of their generosity. It makes them feel great! Being charitable does amazing things for the self-esteem.) Actually, it isn't selfish, nor egoistic, to look out for our own best interests. On the contrary, it provides the foundation for being generous to others.

To receive everything, one must open one's hands and give. TAISIN DESHIMARU

Nonetheless, many of us have been taught that self-love is negative and narcissistic. In reality, it is just the opposite. People with self-love feel nurtured and complete, and they have something left over for other people as well.

The idea that each of us has intrinsic value is part of many religions. The idea that each of us is equal in the eyes of God encompasses not only our intrinsic value, but the idea that at a fundamental level we all have the same value. The democratic principal is the political embodiment of this idea. Self-assertiveness is the social principal. And valuing ourselves is the inner, personal embodiment.

Self-love, my liege, is not so vile a sin
As self-neglecting. SHAKESPEARE

Self-love does not cause us to behave in ways that will lower our self-respect or create shame, because those feelings do nothing for us. Self-love makes us feel good because it makes us behave in ways that are good.

On the other hand, self-hate can certainly cause us to do things that the world will brand as heartless and selfish. Self-hate limits our responses to life, because we always have to be on the lookout for ways to protect our shaky self-esteem. Self-hate causes resistance, and stiffness, and an inability to think about anyone else's pain. It takes a strong sense of self-love to be able to forget yourself for even a little while.

When we understand that the secret of happiness lies not in possessing but in giving, by making others happy we shall be happier ourselves. ANDRÉ GIDE

It is arrogant to be too hard on ourselves. Thinking "It's all my fault" means we're on a power trip. In a bizarre way, it can actually make us feel stronger to be angry at ourselves, as though we were "above" ourselves. We choose to blame ourselves rather than admit that our self-hate has given us fewer options than we might otherwise have.

She faced the crowd and cried:
I love you all but one:
the one who wears my face.
She is the one I fled from.

DILYS LAING

To get our self-esteem back, we have to take a few steps that may not seem very realistic. For one thing, we have to accept that we have the right to be respected, protected, encouraged, and loved. Next, we have to transcend our society, at least to some extent. What that means is that we achieve emotional independence, or detachment, from outside influences, including other people.

It is a funny thing about life; if you refuse to accept anything but the best, you very often get it.

SOMERSET MAUGHAM

The self-valuing person responds to his inner callings and interprets for himself what his basic way of being in the world should be. That might include reinterpreting the way he relates to others, to his work, to his spouse, his religion, and even a renewed definition of himself and his basic place in the scheme of things. This is not to be feared, for the self-valuing person begins to act through a fresh and truly generous perspective. He is not going to do anything to hurt himself, as all miserly actions eventually do.

This takes courage, more so at first than later, when it has shown itself to be so right that we can't imagine falling back into self-hatred. But at first it takes courage to live in a way that honors what is inside us.

> ***Wholeness exists to the extent an individual is conscious of and receptive to his innermost self. The more aware and accepting a person becomes of his inner images and motivations, the more he becomes healed.***
>
> MARSHA SINETAR

In the practice of valuing ourselves, our personalities become enriched and gain power. We learn who we really are, and we awaken to our needs and wants. We also become able—and willing—to act out our real selves in our lives.

Knowing the truth about ourselves may mean discovering a need to stretch into untried, frighteningly difficult arenas, however, and that is where courage comes into play. Some decisions will sting; some will mean adjusting how we live. We may have to change familiar routines or shuffle familiar concerns. Sometimes we have to *seemingly* hurt others in our "selfish" growth toward self-love. But only *seemingly,* because relationships based on self-hatred are not honest or beneficial to either party. In the end, a temporary hurt of this kind leads to greater growth and freedom for everyone involved.

On the other hand, when we are afraid to exercise self-love, we are held in check, stunted, even crippled. The longer our fear persists, the more we hate ourselves, and the more passively we live, unable to express what we need or know what we want. In the end, all our relationships are reflections of our relationship with ourselves. Which means that the most important relationship in our lives is with ourselves.

Self-esteem is the most valuable of the emotions.

FRANK MOORE COLBY

Still, self-esteem is a difficult idea. It requires us to attack those automatic thoughts we have which work to undermine us. The critic within us is remarkably resourceful. It tends to strike, then like the small snake it is, flick into a crack in the rocks. It may take years to silence the voices of self-blame, self-denigration, and self-hate, and learn to speak encouragingly to ourselves.

We have to have the courage to be ourselves. When we listen to our inner callings, when we do what Deepak Chopra calls "following our bliss," we are practicing the art of self-love. The self-affirming life requires will: the will to have more life, to surpass ourselves. Finding out what we really want, and having the courage to be, do, and have what we want, requires facing the enemy within and without.

When any real progress is made, we unlearn and learn anew what we thought we knew before.

HENRY DAVID THOREAU

AFFIRMATION

I am more valuable to myself and to the world when I choose self-love over self-hate.

TO THINK AND WRITE ABOUT

If you are timid about loving yourself, journal work may help solve the problem. The journal is a perfect place to practice self-love. In the process, you may recognize that a large part of your fear lies in actively admitting that you deserve to love yourself.

You can alter undesirable patterns of self-talk through imaginatively rehearsing alternative patterns in your journal. For example, visualize yourself as a person who values herself. What would you say to yourself? How would you behave in your daily routines? If there is someone who seems actively interested in making you hate yourself, who regularly treats you like an erring dog called to heel, what should you say to him?

Begin a process of self-reprogramming—and learn to love yourself.

Part Two

Putting Ourselves First

Chapter 3

Choosing to Be Cheerful

Sunshine in the House

Things do not change; we change.

HENRY DAVID THOREAU

It is the natural order of things that for every action there is an equivalent reaction. For every moment of elation there is a letdown; for every drunken high there is a hangover; for every hour in which our glands pour out elixirs of pleasant moods, there comes an hour when those glands must rest. In the dust of everyday human existence, feelings tire and enthusiasms wane. Is that any reason to cry that life is a snare and all happiness is an illusion? Just because the bubbles stop rising in the glass of champagne? We can't avoid certain hours—or days, or, yes, even months—of feeling low. There's nothing mysterious about it, and nothing that should give us an excuse for self-pity.

Yet many of us approach our lives with unhappy minds, and that *is* pitiable, since choosing to be cheerful is completely possible for the normal, mentally healthy person.

Men are disturbed not by things but by the views which they take of them. EPICTETUS

Life is short, and we all want to reap our share of happiness, but "happy" is one of those words that means very different things to different people. If we mean "delight," "glee," "exaltation," then it's likely we will be able to count our "happy" moments in life on our fingers. If we are realistic and admit that moments of pure delight are rare, then we can better define "happy" as a feeling of contentment and cheerfulness. That kind of happiness is never loud. It doesn't shout in the streets.

I have always preferred Cheerfulness to Mirth. The latter I consider as an Act, the former as a Habit of the Mind. Mirth is short and transient, Cheerfulness fixed and permanent.

JOSEPH ADISON

Habitual cheerfulness has two strong arguments: It is a better staging ground for launches into moments of pure delight since it is already relatively high on the mood scale. And it can be cultivated as a habit.

But no happiness can settle on an adult unless he gives it permission to settle. William James said that the greatest discovery of his time was that human beings could alter their lives by altering their attitudes of mind. We will feel temporarily "down" at times, but the habitually cheerful person does not let this fact control her.

Let us train our minds to desire what the situation demands. SENECA

There are a lot of melancholy people in the world. Their dejection leads them to expect little from life, and that is exactly what they get. On the other hand, a habit of cheerfulness can have a powerful effect. We know there is an intimate correlation between mental health and physical health, for instance. And people who get control of their minds and resolve to be cheerful often can beat even deadly diseases.

One way to encourage a cheerful mind-set is to accept that we aren't going to have moments of ecstasy on a daily basis, that we will feel low now and then, and to resolve not to let these facts control our resolve to be cheerful.

> ***A happy woman is one who has no cares at all; a cheerful woman is one who has cares but doesn't let them get her down.***
>
> BEVERLY SILLS

This doesn't mean that we have to take pleasure in our lows, nor do we have to steel ourselves against them. Instead, it means that we acknowledge that we feel low, tell ourselves, "This too will pass," and get on with our lives. We don't wear our depression on our sleeves, hoping for sympathy. We put on a smile and relate to the world in the same way we do when we are more effortlessly cheerful.

The happy secret behind this behavior is that acting as if we are cheerful often will make us cheerful. Yes, the mind can affect the body, but it isn't so well-known that the body can equally affect the mind. Putting on a smile, walking with our heads up, speaking in a cheerful way, can ultimately create cheerfulness in our minds. Just as behavior follows emotion, emotion follows behavior. And by regulating our behavior, which is largely under the control of our willpower, we can indirectly regulate our emotions. Therefore, a voluntary route to cheerfulness is to sit up and perform and speak *as if we were* cheerful.

Our habits of mind are easily rusted in place. Our tendency is to place them in gear at an early stage and then leave them there. In order to shift to a higher sprocket, we might need to use a rough file on occasion. We might need to get tough with ourselves, to force ourselves to behave cheerfully once or twice in order to prove just how worthwhile the effort is.

> ***The growth of the human mind is still high adventure, in many ways the highest adventure on earth.***
> NORMAN COUSINS

This kind of resolved cheerfulness is based on hope and courage: As long as we can hope that our lows are only temporary, we can generate the courage necessary to hang on. Life, however, sometimes offers us a terrible uphill climb, and our hope and courage get short of breath. One way to generate reserve supplies for hard times is to take time each day to think about everything we have to be grateful for. The list is bound to be long, encompassing everyone we love, everything we have, and even our nonmaterial blessings, like sitting in a room full of the sunset's color, watching romantic movies through blurring tears, and listening to the extraordinary voices of children at play.

If we practice gratitude and celebration for what we already have, then we will always have reserves of hope and courage for the difficult times.

> ***You ought to be glad about your life, whatever it is. I've got all my fingers and toes. My eyesight is***

good. My smeller works. Of course I'm happy about my life, because I'm still here.

MORGAN FREEMAN

Sometimes, of course, we have every good reason to feel absolutely miserable. Grief and real, physical pain are two examples of perfectly excusable reasons for us to feel disheartened. But again, there are people who somehow manage to function as if they are cheerful even in the midst of grief and pain. Consider Viktor Frankl, who wrote about his imprisonment in a concentration camp in *Man's Search for Meaning*. He wrote about "the last of human freedoms"—our ability to choose our attitude in any given set of circumstances. Not all of us are perhaps so courageous at our core, just as not everyone who came under the horror of the Holocaust bore up so well as those Frankl used as shining examples. Still, surely we can try to measure up in our daily dealings with life.

One must be pitiless about this matter of mood.

JOYCE CAROL OATES

On the other hand, some of us are terribly sensitive to the least verbal criticism or barbed dart of bad feeling, and we use that as an excuse to pity ourselves and greet the world with despair. This is self-indulgence. Such people believe their moods are inflicted on them by the world rather than recognizing that they are the inflictors. In reality, they make an agreement with unhappiness. It is as if they walk under an umbrella of unhappiness and say, "See, this is how I live." That umbrella becomes their reality. For those of us who are living among these umbrella-carriers, it is time to wake up and step out of the shade and into the sun. And by simply acknowledging our interest in making a change, we are conveyed to the next step on our journey.

We must avoid using our moods as excuses. We must master our moods, or else our moods will master us. Even if we feel we have a legitimate cause for unhappiness, it is up to us to either seek solutions or seek professional help.

We can shift those rusty gears and change negative mental perspectives when we acknowledge that the viewpoint we choose is vital to our moods. And to a large extent, our viewpoint is a matter of choice. Our thoughts and our moods are linked, and when we change one we also change the other. Choosing to be cheerful improves our mood. How? By changing our thinking.

> ***Happiness is the only good. The place to be happy is here. The time to be happy is now.***
>
> ROBERT INGERSOLL

We are the thinkers of our own thoughts. Thinking isn't something that happens to us. Rather, thinking is something that we *do*. In order to redirect the thoughts that we are thinking when we're feeling down, the first question to ask is, "Is there another way of seeing things?"

Here is an example: In January, John's wife was given a chance to travel to Hawaii. John planned to go with her. Then his workload suddenly increased, and it became obvious that he couldn't go after all. At that moment, John stood at a fork in the road. If he took the direction most commonly traveled, he would fall into a black mood, and feel hopeless and defeated. Choosing this direction, John asked, "What's the use?" He concentrated on the negative, giving himself up to his "problem." His wife's ability to enjoy the trip was marred by his disappointment. After her departure, John used his disappointment to rationalize his grumpy behavior at work. As spatters of hail rapped the glass window of his office, he thought enviously of the sunny beach where his wife was lounging, and he felt resentful of her pleasure.

That was the easiest response for John to take, partly because he had seen so many others take it before him. Feeling victimized takes very little effort.

> ***I unconsciously decided that, even if it wasn't an ideal world, it should be and so painted only the ideal aspects of it, pictures in which there are no drunken slatterns or self-centered mothers . . . only foxy grandpas who played baseball with the kids and boys who fished from logs and got up circuses in the backyard.***
>
> NORMAN ROCKWELL

John could, however, take another road. He could see his wife off with a smile and harness his unhappiness and turn it into opportunity, to enjoy time with friends, perhaps even host a casual poker party while his wife was away, or spend time with his sister, whom his wife didn't get along with. He might even use his empty evenings to analyze how he could reorganize his work so that surprise increases in his workload wouldn't occur again. In other words, he could keep his perspective, focus on retrieval, and look for possibilities, even for growth opportunities. He could then take pride in calling on his inner reservoirs of strength instead of making everyone else pay for his disappointment.

We must remember not to be so determined to get what

we want from life that we miss lessons to be learned from less than blissful events. There is always more than one way of seeing things. If we accept that fact, then our only remaining difficulty is to find other points of view to choose from. A low-level perspective is bound to be most ready to hand. So how can we step back and see the other choices available to us?

> ***I went out to Charing Cross, to see Major-General Harrison hanged, drawn, and quartered; which was done there, he looking as cheerful as any man could do in that condition.*** SAMUEL PEPYS

This is no shallow recommendation of "cockeyed optimism" or "always look on the bright side." Developing the habit of searching for different and wider perspectives helps us to cope realistically and flexibly with difficulties as they arise. It gives us more options.

Our very process of thinking—what we think about, what we remember, how we see things—is altered by our moods. The problem is that a bad mood brings about bad thoughts, so the mood gets worse, bringing worse thoughts, and so on, in a vicious cycle. If we were to think differently, or adopt another point of view, we would begin to feel differently. This is the key. We can tackle our thoughts as a way of tackling our moods.

It may help to think back and pinpoint the specific moment when we first noticed feeling bad. That makes the task of identifying the first bad thoughts easier. Doing this habitually is like becoming an expert mechanic who can listen to the sound of a car's engine, watch how it performs, and then narrow down the possible sources of trouble.

'Tis easy enough to be pleasant,
When life flows along like a song;
But the man worth while is the one who will smile
When everything goes dead wrong.

ELLA WHEELER WILCOX

It is often difficult to narrow down what thoughts are in our minds. Sometimes they are subverbal—that is, not easily put into words. Or they can be so familiar that they "go without saying." In that case, we may also need to consider our beliefs, attitudes, ideas, images—all the contents of our mind, including our dreams. Along with rusty gears, our minds can hold a lot of assumptions we haven't tested in a long while. We can ask ourselves, "What went through my mind at the time?" "How am I seeing things now?" "What is it about this that matters to me?" "What does this mean to me? About me?"

Then we can look for alternates that may make us feel more cheerful. We can arrive at a plan of action. As a result, we'll feel much better.

There is always more than one way of seeing things. Although we may not always be able to choose the facts of our lives, we can always choose how we react to them. We can help ourselves maintain a steady cheerfulness by looking at the facts from a cheerful perspective. The first step is to understand the way thoughts and moods link. The second step is to examine our thoughts and see which perspective we are operating under. By changing our thoughts, we can change our perspective. Finding new perspectives gives us more options and helps us choose to be cheerful.

Happiness is no laughing matter.

RICHARD WHATELY

AFFIRMATION

Every aspect of my life is, in a sense, a vote for the kind of world I want to live in; therefore I will be cheerful, for the sake of a more pleasant world.

TO THINK AND WRITE ABOUT

If blocks to cheerfulness seem to reside in your past, it is beneficial to unveil these blocks in your journal. When fighting a blue mood, record your memories of when you first felt this way. Using your imagination, try to put yourself back into that time and place. What sights and sounds accompanied the moment?

At first, your remembrance may be incomplete. Dilate what you have, using your senses to build a more complete recall. Try to recreate the memory. Write enough specific details to bring the moment back to life. What did you feel, hear, taste, see? Describe what you were thinking, even what your body felt like at that time.

Once you have reproduced the moment in writing, you can consider it at your leisure. Are you still that person? Would you react the same way today? Ask yourself the questions suggested in the text above.

Remember, the object is not to relive the moment—this is not an exercise in wallowing—but to put your memory into the perspective of who you are and what your life is now.

Chapter 4

Asserting Ourselves

Casting Aside That Fictitious Self That We Assume Like a Garment

I grew up pretty much as everybody else grows up, and one day . . . found myself saying to myself—I can't live where I want to—I can't go where I want to—I can't do what I want to—I can't even say what I want to . . .

GEORGIA O'KEEFFE

Assertiveness is a skill based on the idea that our needs, wants, and feelings are neither more nor less important than those of other people: They are equally important.

The message of self-assertion for women in the 1970s produced a generation who upset the established status quo. Some relationships were threatened by the idea of women feeling equal, but most men found assertive women of great help in understanding "where women were coming from." Assertive behavior has fostered better understanding and communication between the sexes by easing honesty and freedom. And freedom helps us all attend to and care for the elements of ourselves that make us happy and that help us to become kinder, gentler, more charitable, and loving.

Assertive behavior doesn't aid women alone. It is so effective, it should be the style of choice for everyone. If we have high self-regard, a positive sense of personal value, a capacity for independence, then, whether male or female, we will naturally want to be assertive. Assertive behavior lets us be free to be ourselves.

> ***Self-confidence is the first requisite to great undertakings.*** SAMUEL JOHNSON

If we are new to valuing ourselves, we may be caught between conforming to existing standards in our lives and exploring promising new alternatives. Inevitably, there will be imbalances as we begin to choose some of the new alternatives and attempt to integrate them into our established patterns. For instance, in the 1970s, husbands often objected when their wives chose to attend classes rather than stay home every evening as they always had. The most common first reaction to any change is resistance.

In response, wives of that decade were unhappy to realize that although they had always believed there were no boundaries on their independence, their choices had, after all, been very narrow. They felt angry about being prevented from choosing their own paths. At the same time, they felt helpless to express their feelings directly and spontaneously. They felt powerless to get what they needed and wanted.

Assertive behavior was the way to express these differing viewpoints so that husbands and wives could come to agreeable solutions. (Many marriages failed in the 1970s, but that was not the fault of assertive behavior. Quite the contrary.)

You won't skid if you stay in a rut.

FRANK MCKINNEY HUBBARD

Here are two less dated examples of the need for assertive behavior: Ted finds he can't ask for the return of a borrowed tool from his neighbor without being apologetic. Jeanne can't tell her lover what caresses feel good to her.

In such anxiety-provoking situations, many of us feel unable to act. We find ourselves at a loss to come up with effective action, or any action at all.

But it is our perfect right to express our honest feelings, to be direct and straightforward with them, without experiencing undue anxiety or guilt ourselves. We can exercise our personal rights without denying the rights of others by being assertive.

Trust thyself: every heart vibrates to that iron string.

RALPH WALDO EMERSON

A nonassertive person expends a lot of energy avoiding conflicts, manipulating others, and denying responsibility for her own actions. On the other hand, the aggressive person may act to resolve conflicts or to achieve goals while violating the rights of others. Neither style is healthy or helpful. Learning to be assertive is the answer. Self-assertion is as basic as food, shelter, and love. Without these essentials, there is eventual death—either physical, spiritual, or emotional.

There is so much more to be gained from life by being free and able to stand up for oneself, and from honoring the same right for others.

ROBERT E. ALBERTI AND MICHAEL L. EMMONS

If we think about it, there are three modes, or styles, of behavior we can identify in ourselves when examining our conduct in various social situations. They are passive, aggressive, or assertive. Let's use the common situation of parenting to show the differences in these styles.

We may become aggressive with our children at times, and overreact to them. Maybe we do this more often when we come home frustrated over feeling like a patsy in some work situation. So we overcompensate when we get home. A simple matter of spilled milk, and we feel as if something is going to pop, rip, or split.

Or, if passiveness is the parent's regular style, she may spoil her children with a shoe-clerk willingness to please. It may be her coworkers who get this person's anger. Of course, neither style is beneficial. Aggressive parents tend to squelch their children; passive parents force their children into taking responsibility for their own decisions prematurely. But when we haven't achieved balance, our behavior is likely to swing between opposite extremes.

Our goal as assertive parents is to encourage assertiveness in our children. We want to acknowledge their rights as much as possible. But when we do make a decision, we state it clearly: This is what I want you to do.

Aggressive behavior may not always be overt. Sometimes we smile as we stab others in the back, or give compliments that are really subtle put-downs, or get our own way by manipulation. Even when it is indirect, however, aggression is aggression.

When she is angry, she is likely to use sneaky ways to get revenge. She can be so indirect that the person with whom she is angry may never even know that she was angry or what her anger was about.

STANLEE PHELPS AND NANCY AUSTIN

Many of us are so used to passive or aggressive patterns, we are unaware that there is an alternative way to respond to people and situations. With practice, we can incorporate assertive skills comfortably into our own styles.

> ***The great thing in the world is not so much where we are but in what direction we are going.***
>
> OLIVER WENDELL HOLMES

Because all learning is a very personal experience, it is necessary for us first to know ourselves so that we can adapt assertive techniques to our own needs. For example, Todd, who was single, gave up career opportunities to take care of his parents, who frequently reminded him of how old and infirm they were. He felt unable to be assertive with his parents, who had reared him to meet the needs of others before his own. Todd was being manipulated into exercising compassion. Manipulation involves particularly devious or indirect methods of aggression to induce someone to behave in a certain manner. It is the use of dishonest means to achieve a desired goal. Emotional blackmail, such as Todd's parents were using, is a classic example of the manipulative process.

> ***The Queen turned crimson with fury, and after glaring at [Alice] for a moment like a wild beast, began screaming, "Off with her head! Off with—"***
>
> ***"Nonsense!" said Alice, and the Queen was silent.***
>
> LEWIS CARROLL

Many of us have been taught that we exist to serve others, to provide tenderness and compassion to everyone (except ourselves) at all times. This attitude is very difficult to throw off. In acting out what is expected of us, we feel our intentions are honorable, and frankly, there is some satisfaction in that, but if we are unable to express our concerns for ourselves, that satisfaction won't be enough.

Todd always said yes to his parents' needs, because he didn't want to risk upsetting them. He needed to remember *his* feelings. Courageously, he finally presented his dilemma to his parents, however hollow in the heart it made him feel. He had an unprecedented opportunity to advance in his job, but he had to move to do it. He offered to help his parents to move with him, so that he could continue to care for them while seeing to his own future as well. After a shocked silence, not surprisingly, they responded with resistance to his new assertiveness. Eventually, however, they saw his resolve, and agreed to the move.

That was when Todd told himself, "I'm not very nice."

To short-circuit rebound guilt, we need to consider the price we pay when we do things at the expense of our own happiness. And we need to be aware of the negative self-labels we may attach to our assertive behavior. Then we can work toward replacing those labels with more positive ones.

> ***One's philosophy is not best expressed in words, it is expressed in the choices one makes . . . In the long run, we shape our lives and we shape ourselves. The process never ends until we die. And the choices we make are ultimately our responsibility.***
>
> ELEANOR ROOSEVELT

In order to become more assertive, we must grow more conscious of our own habits and thought processes and decide which of those can further our growth and which will delay it. In practicing assertiveness, we will probably run up against timeworn standards in ourselves that we acquired long ago. If we learned to behave passively, we may fear saying the wrong thing: People will think we're stupid. Or we may be so habitually passive that we feel it is aggressive to assert ourselves. We are probably used to having only two alternatives—continue to behave passively and obediently, or retreat completely from the situation.

Neither of those alternatives is a solution. We have to recognize that by asserting ourselves we will eventually feel better, and that by expressing our views, we benefit without harming anyone else. The goal of assertion is not victory, but being able to express our needs and desires openly and honestly.

Self-expression must pass into communication for its fulfillment.

PEARL S. BUCK

The need for approval prevents many of us from developing any sense of power. Apology and powerlessness characterize our lives. For instance, how many of us apologize when someone steps on *our* foot? Far too many! Reasonable and proper occasions for apologies abound, but this is not one of them. The next time we apologize for anything, we should ask ourselves what we are apologizing for. And we should start keeping count of how many times we say, "I'm sorry" inappropriately.

The greatest mistake you can make in life is to be continually fearing that you will make one.

ELBERT HUBBARD

Suppressed anger is often at the root of aggressive behavior. Taking responsibility for ourselves is a quality of maturity, and that means taking responsibility for our anger as well.

As we grow and become aware, we may realize that we have accumulated years of anger. We may be lumbering through our lives expressing this anger subtly and at random. If we were porcupines, our prickles could hardly be more evident. Yet though we "needle" others in casually arbitrary ways, at the same time we feel that any overt expression of anger is taboo. We are trained to hold back our negative feelings. Anger is a powerful emotion, however, and it is difficult to suppress. It is also a driving force of energy and can be expressed appropriately.

Recognizing anger is the first step toward learning how to deal with it. As we locate those emotions, we can begin to pinpoint their origins. Knowing the facts about our anger helps us set its parameters.

Good judgment needs to be exercised, too. The best way is to state anger is directly: "I'm angry about . . . " Even children can understand that.

> ***The worst thing one can do is not to try, to be aware of what one wants and not give in to it, to spend years in silent hurt wondering if something could have materialized—and never knowing.***
>
> DAVID S. VISCOTT

It is normal to feel uncomfortable as we change to a more assertive manner, especially if people near us sense that it means they must change as well. To counteract that, we need to solicit the support of the people with whom we are intimate. The help of reassuring allies will speed up our growth.

Meanwhile, we must go on exploring direct alternatives of relating to everyone while respecting our own feelings as well as theirs.

If I am not for myself, who will be for me? If I am not for others, who am I for? And if not now, when?

TALMUD

AFFIRMATION

I can grow ever more self-assertive by working on it, surviving my mistakes, and celebrating my successes.

TO THINK AND WRITE ABOUT

Has there been a road you did not take earlier in life because you felt inhibited or unable to assert your wishes? Keep in mind that such an early rejection of a path may have been an intimation of abilities or talents that needed more time to develop. Are you ready now? Are you ready to assert your desire to correct this wrong?

As a first step, imagine what your life would be now if you had taken that passed-by route. Imagine what your future will be like if you were to take the route now.

The aim of exploring rejected roads is not to wallow in "if only" sentiments. You can't really know what actually would have happened if you had taken another path. But by reviewing important intersections, you may uncover future options.

Recalling past forks in the road and working with them in your journal can be therapeutic, liberating, instructive—or just entertaining. And the road not followed may still lead to a point in your future.

Part Three

Sharing Ourselves

Chapter 5

FRIENDSHIPS

O Who Will Walk a Mile with Me?

I breathed a song into the air,
It fell to earth, I knew not where . . .

HENRY WADSWORTH LONGFELLOW

If we offer something of ourselves to the world—a good deed, a kind word, our love—eventually we will discover its effects. It may come back to us in the form of a friend. But the word "friendship" tends to be one of those stained-glass words, like "goodness," "fate," and "innocence." It tends to be idealized and sentimentalized until the reality feels somehow lacking.

The simplest definition of a friend is someone we want to be with. But friends can also be helpmates. After all, we are here to help each other along.

Having a friend is just one side of the relationship. However, it is the side with which we most consciously concern ourselves. *Being* a friend is usually more important to our development.

Sometimes, what we go through for a friend leaves us slightly worn and torn, but that's what makes a friendship real. Enduring friends stick together through adversity, give a little bit more than they expect to receive, and encourage each other to do more than they would have done alone. New friendships bring us pleasure, and old friendships comfort us.

The Christian Bible tells of a widow's decision to leave her homeland and travel to Judah with her Hebrew mother-in-law. Ruth's words to Naomi are one of our greatest statements of friendship.

> ***Whither thou goest, I will go; and where thou lodgest, I will lodge: thy people shall be my people, and thy God my god. Where thou diest, will I die, and there will be buried.*** THE BOOK OF RUTH

Ruth's vow may be a bit steep for most of us, yet in our friendships we see a paradigm for all our human relations. Every time we offer friendship to someone, we strengthen the bonds of brotherhood and sisterhood for all. The ancient Greeks understood that the health of the community depended on how well its individual citizens treated each other. They listed friendship among the highest of virtues. It was considered an essential element in a fully flourishing life.

Even in this modern world of perishable relationships, our friendships are worth tending. According to Aristotle, there are three basic kinds of friendship: those based on pleasure in another's company, those based on usefulness, and those based on mutual admiration. All are basic to the good life, and the best of friends will not only admire each other, but will take pleasure in each other's company, *and* find their association to be of mutual advantage.

Yet it doesn't always happen that we get all three benefits from one friendship. Such a relationship is more likely to develop in marriage, since it is more properly a form of love. In fact, Aristotle termed this three-faceted relationship "loving friendship."

Thomas Jefferson and James Madison met in 1776 and from then on they marched in step, arms swinging in unison, as they worked together to further the American Revolution and shape a new scheme of government. From their work sprang a friendship of incomparable collaboration. It lasted fifty years. Still, it was probably not the embodiment of that perfect friendship described by Aristotle. Although they probably felt some mutual admiration, mostly they shared purpose—a common end—and a knowledge that in joining forces they both could benefit.

Cicero defined friendship as a complete identity and agreement about all things, an identity and agreement strengthened by mutual goodwill and affection. That definition seems almost utopian in its expectations. Like Aristotle's loving friendship, is it asking too much of friendship?

> ***I do not wish to treat friendships daintily, but with roughest courage. When they are real, they are not glass threads or frostwork, but the solidest thing we know.*** RALPH WALDO EMERSON

Friendships customarily arise out of mutual interests or common aims, and these pursuits are then strengthened by the generous impulses of each person involved. On occasion that loving friendship spoken of by Aristotle may come into being. But we shouldn't expect it.

A great friendship was shared by Helen Keller and Anne

Sullivan. Illness destroyed Helen's sight and hearing before she was two years old, leaving her cut off from the world. For the next five years she grew up wild and unruly. Anne Sullivan's arrival changed Helen's life. Anne herself was half-blind from an eye infection, and she came to Helen with experience, unbending dedication, and love. Through the sense of touch she was able to make contact with the young girl's mind, and in the next three years she taught Helen to read and write in braille.

> ***'Tis the human touch in this world that counts,***
> ***The touch of your hand and mine . . .***
>
> SPENCER MICHAEL FREE

By sixteen, Helen could speak well enough to go to preparatory school and college. She graduated *cum laude* from Radcliffe in 1904, and devoted the rest of her life to helping the blind and the deaf-blind. The two women continued their remarkable friendship until Anne's death.

Their friendship tells us that these infrequent relationships are about the closeness of hands, hearts, and souls. Their example—its frankness, its opportunities for self-revelation, its ability to listen to criticism as earnestly as praise, its stand-by-me loyalty, and even its self-sacrifice—is potent encouragement to develop our own friendships to their fullest flowering.

Yet we must understand that all friendships, whether of the profound nature of Helen Keller and Anne Sullivan's or of the more moderate nature we enjoy ordinarily, will have their ups and downs. On either side of a friendship stands a separate individual leading a complex life, growing in very personal directions. Friendships work best if we are able to be ourselves within them. Learning to allow for disparity makes our companionship more likely to last.

> ***So many qualities are requisite to the possibility of friendship and so many accidents must concur to its rise and continuance, that the greatest part of mankind content themselves without it.***
>
> SAMUEL JOHNSON

Also, sometimes it happens that the obligations of friendship compete with other obligations and affections. And as people grow and change, through no fault of anyone, certain friendships lose their basis and slip into the realm of acquaintanceship. Attempting to preserve the intensity of a relationship that no longer fits only bends both sides out of shape. If we have to suppress our growth because of the fixed structure of a friendship, then we are stunting both ourselves and our friend. A stubborn commitment to an outgrown alliance will cause us to neglect other ways in which each of us could be nourishing ourselves.

This is not to condone using people and then tossing them away. Nor does it mean that we shouldn't be willing to help a friend through difficult times. But most of us have had friendships lose their core of common feeling. In the normal course, both sides mutually agree to less and less frequent meetings. This is not something we should suffer undue guilt about, despite the sentimentality that gives us commercials and essays about lifelong associations. Occasionally these super-friendships do happen, but they are rare.

> ***Two friendships in two breasts requires***
> ***The same aversions and desires.*** JONATHAN SWIFT

We all wish we could have at least one lifelong friend of that sort, yet, outside of marriage (and too often not even there) we really aren't likely to find an individual with whom we're absolutely compatible in our tastes, values, attitudes, and ideas.

Which doesn't mean we can't benefit greatly from the friendships we're far more likely to make—with individuals with whom we have one or more things in common. Forwarding those relationships can make our lives quite interesting enough. Such friendships furnish us with that marvelous feeling of reassurance that at least some of our viewpoints, pleasures, and concerns are shared by others.

Therefore, a realistic approach informs us that each friendship we have should be taken on its own merits. It should be allowed to evolve as it will—with no preconceived goals, structure, expectations, or rules. For instance, we don't have to share uncommon interests with a friend; in fact, we are better off limiting each relationship to the enjoyment of the things we do have in common.

The best advice is to take things as they are. Friendships don't have to be structured, perpetuated, and tied down. They work out best if we let them unfold as they will, limiting our expectations to what is, and continues to be, mutually beneficial to both sides.

Friendship cannot live with ceremony, nor without civility. LORD HALIFAX

When we find a friend who is intellectually stimulating, we should enjoy her for the excellent discussions we can have. We certainly shouldn't expect that friend to help us rearrange our furniture or lend us money. Those things are separate parts of our lives. Friendships shouldn't be burdened with the impossible expectation of encompassing all our needs. And they won't be if we don't try to tie them down with illogical obligations, loyalties, duties, commitments, or appeals for sympathy. If we are going to develop our own selves, then let's make it a policy to allow everyone else to do so as well.

If we can let others be as free as we wish to be, then we *will* be rare and valuable friends. We'll be in demand because we won't create conflicts and arguments.

> ***Treat your friends as you do your pictures, and place them in their best light.***
>
> JENNIE JEROME CHURCHILL

If we treat our friendships with respect, we will be sensitive to clues that they may no longer be mutually nourishing. Sometimes small conflicts can be settled with candid and self-assertive communication. But sometimes camaraderie will naturally fade into acquaintanceship. Hanging onto a friendship that no longer serves, though it may have started with an ecstatic glow, can engulf us in hurt feelings, resentment, and arguments.

This seems to happen more often to women, who are by nature relationship-keepers. Beth began her friendship with Joan when both were young mothers with a desire to become artists. As time passed, it became more apparent that these facts were the only things they shared in common. The values they held in their personal lives varied drastically. For instance, when Joan had an extramarital affair, Beth was appalled.

> ***I was fixed there, imbedded in time, imbedded in a life I had in some curious way outgrown.***
>
> JOHN D. MACDONALD

But the two still had art in common. Since friendship to the isolated artist is valuable beyond measure, that aspect of their association remained a source of pleasure for many years. They agreed that they would crawl miles over broken glass for any sign of success. But when Beth's work actually began to sell, Joan's reaction was to subtly sabotage her confidence. In the guise of encouraging Beth to do her best work, she hinted that Beth's current work was tawdry. Beth felt unable to respond for fear of appearing self-important in her growing success. The relationship went on this way for several years, its surface of rapport becoming thinner and thinner as deeper feelings of frustration and resentment grew up from the depths. It finally ended with a phone call when Joan told Beth that a current piece of her work was "embarrassing." Beth's silence hovered ominously for a long moment; then she asked Joan not to call her again.

> ***Relationships can be fruitful only when they're in the self-interest of each person. Unfortunately, the normal labels and assumptions go far beyond that, and so problems develop.*** HARRY BROWNE

Why do such things happen? Our expectations concerning the role of a friend may be the problem. Both women in the above example were caught in a relationship that no longer served either of them. In a perfect world, they might have worked it out in an amenable way, but since this is not a perfect world, the relationship ended bitterly. That was unfortunate, but was it worse than continuing a "friendship" that left each party feeling diminished?

Here is another example. Palmer liked his dorm-mate, Harold. Their relationship was loosely friendly. Then Harold made plans for them to take a midterm vacation together at his grandfather's farm. "You'll love it—never-ending miles of golden wheat." Palmer wasn't interested in wheat, nor was he ready to enlarge this relatively simple and enjoyable relationship. He wanted to be fair to Harold, but he had a right to his own feelings and opinions. So he told Harold that he didn't feel comfortable with the idea. Harold's first reaction was hurt (resistance), but in the end, he went on his vacation without Palmer. When he returned, the two continued as loosely friendly roommates—really the perfect relationship for living together in a dorm situation.

> ***Living the truth in your heart without compromise brings kindness into the world. Attempts at kindness that compromise your heart cause only sadness.***
>
> ANONYMOUS EIGHTEENTH-CENTURY MONK

The lesson of these stories is that we must treat friendships, new and old, with care. We shouldn't force a friendship to be an end in itself, something that must be perpetuated at all costs. We shouldn't ask for sacrifices in the name of friendship. We shouldn't add inappropriate activities, try to fit it within a preconceived context, or add obligations incompatible with its context. We *should* let each friendship evolve as mutual enjoyment and self-nourishment dictates.

For the most part, each of our friends will connect with only one or two parts of our lives. We might enjoy bowling with Judy. That doesn't mean we should combine our children, parents, and in-laws with hers for a picnic.

We are better to enter friendship cautiously, expecting only to enjoy what we have in common. Any enlargement of the relationship should take place with equal caution and with awareness that we might be opening a door to conflicts. To avoid that, we should feel free to say no to such enlargements with assurance.

Good friends inspire us, bad friends stifle us. We must always be mindful of our own and our friends' interests and give one another room to grow. We don't want to wall in our friends, or let ourselves be similarly walled.

> ***He would walk into my mind as if it were a town and be a torchlight procession of one, lighting up the streets . . .***
>
> EULOGY BY ONE FRIEND FOR ANOTHER, QUOTED BY SEAMUS HEANEY

AFFIRMATION

I will be a friend and I will make friends without idealizing what friendship normally offers.

TO THINK AND WRITE ABOUT

Analyze any present conflicts you have with friends. Identify your assumptions about friendship. Do you need to revise your expectations of your friends? Or their expectations of you?

If you have a troublesome friendship, write out two forecasts of the future, given the continuance or discontinuance of the friendship. What do these projections tell you to do now?

Always return to the present moment, the now. That is your place of power, because the potential for changing the future lies only in the present. If you stay true to the present moment, you will always thrive.

Chapter 6

FORGING A MARRIAGE

Bone of My Bones, and Flesh of My Flesh

Reader, I married him.

CHARLOTTE BRONTË

Love. Such a small word for such a complex idea. How can the concept of love be expressed in a single syllable? How can four letters mean absolutely everything? Even if we could understand love at first sight, how do we explain the kind of love that keeps two people looking at each other that way for years?

One of the bad jokes of evolution is that we have evolved brains which can imagine a state of perfection we cannot achieve. DIANE ACKERMAN

Sometimes, of course, love falters. There is probably no subject as emotionally charged as that of "the sanctity of marriage." Love, closeness, affection, opportunity for family—can these things really be enjoyed over the long term with only one other person?

Though marriage is nearly universal for humans, practiced by just about every culture throughout history, it is no longer a social necessity in this country. Even the moral dictates supporting the "institution" have broken down. A marriage today depends on a man and woman's feelings for each other. Feelings being volatile, marriage has become volatile.

Yet we are left with a need to have and rear children, and more than ever we need companionship and communication in a technical environment and fragmented world. What are we supposed to do?

Nobody knows. We're still getting married, and with the best of intentions, but our floundering, our bafflement, and our failure should come as no surprise. We can feel more certain about our chances of staying married, however, if we understand that we must learn to protect the love we feel on our wedding day.

Though our married love may have begun as infatuation, and though our courtship may have been filled with romance, to endure the daily wear and tear of marriage, love must be stronger than either infatuation or romance. If such a love sounds less than dreamy, those who have been married long and happily tell us it is in reality the deepest bond possible between two people.

> ***Two pure souls fused into one by an impassioned love—friends, counselors—a mutual support and inspiration to each other amid life's struggles, must know the highest human happiness; —this is marriage; and this is the only corner-stone of an enduring home.***
>
> ELIZABETH CADY STANTON

To outsiders, a good, long-term marriage may appear dull, even homely, but to the participants, it is probably the core of their lives. Their partnership may be something to which romance is just a prelude.

Women and men have to fight together to change society—and both will benefit. [My husband and I] are strongly pro-marriage. I think it is a grave mistake for young girls to think that it has to be a career versus marriage, equality versus love. Partnership, not dependence, is the real romance in marriage.

MURIEL FOX

The husband in such a marriage probably doesn't arrange weekly intimate dinners or annual second honeymoons. He may rarely bring his wife flowers. What he may do is keep her car repaired and full of gas so she will never be stranded, and vacuum the carpet when his mother is coming—not because he cares, but because he knows his wife cares. Though Val was not a pet person, when his wife's cat died, he buried the animal for her, held her while she wept, and after a few months, encouraged her to adopt a new kitten. If these efforts weren't "romantic," they certainly were loving. And his wife was wise enough to recognize their significance. True love, the enduring kind, often comes so cleverly disguised that it is easy to overlook.

The vow of fidelity is an absurd commitment, but it is the heart of marriage.

FATHER ROBERT CAPON

Good marriages take nothing less than total commitment. Statistics prove that couples who live together before marriage have an even higher divorce rate than couples who don't try out their marriages first. The idea of trying out marriage seems pretty ridiculous when we think about it—about as logical as biting into an orange to see if we have an appetite for an apple. There is no relationship "like" marriage, and intelligent, self-valuing people aren't going to open the depths of their hearts to a mere experiment. A marriage certificate certainly doesn't solve relationship problems, but until we have the guarantee of one, we can't really begin the struggle of forging two people into one unit, which is the ultimate goal of marriage.

One unit? Does that sound as if after marriage we are to forget things like individual autonomy and independence? Of course not. Rather, a spouse should be a post we can lean on, a person who, when we've really screwed up, loves us anyway. And we should be that kind of a spouse ourselves. That may not sound too difficult, yet it requires a dreadful leap of trust into the realm of intimacy.

> ***Almost all married people fight, although many are ashamed to admit it. Actually a marriage in which no quarreling at all takes place may well be one that is dead or dying from emotional undernourishment. If you care, you probably fight.***
>
> FLORA DAVIS

The first step toward intimacy is communication.

How dry that sounds! How cliché. But in good, lasting marriages, participants talk about everything. They talk daily. When Lisa was having second thoughts about her marriage, she talked to all her friends about her problems. She discussed her husband's failings and her many disappointments with their life together. One friend finally said, "Lisa, we're talking very intimately. Do you talk this way to your husband?" The answer was no. Lisa, like many women, opened herself to intimate and nourishing communication within her friendships, but she expected her marriage to be "romantic." As a result, her friendships were truly loving, while her marriage was cracking right down the middle.

The problem with the romantic ideal is that it ignores the hard work that a good marriage requires. It hints that true love simply knows what is needed to make our lives perfect. We may credit the idea of romance with many of our divorces: We think a good marriage should just "happen." What usually happens is much less dreamy.

It is ironic that historically, when marriages were arranged, people assumed they would get their needs for intimacy fulfilled in friendships. The idea of marriages based on hormones and dating skills is very new and radical. It took lovers centuries to win the right to marry the person with whom they most wished to be intimate. Yet here we are, still working harder to make our friendships more intimate than our marriages.

> ***The American media teach that love is something that happens* to *us, not something we* do. *The phrase "falling in love" implies an accident, not a choice.***
>
> JOHN STOSSEL

Take our wives fishing and share with them our bosom secrets? Meet our husbands for a long lunch and reveal our innermost longings? Start talking and just let the words rush out like air escaping from a punctured tire? Unthinkable? Embarrassing? No, essential! We absolutely must talk and thereby transform our marital relationships into intimate friendships. Love, like friendship, is something we have to make happen. Add the sparks of sexual desire, and we have something excellent. People reporting the greatest satisfaction with life in surveys of happiness are married couples.

Problems will still occur, but now they become something to be attacked mutually. It does take work, however—even more than it used to. Less social insistence that we stay married means we need a greater personal sense of commitment—mate to mate. Sanction-free divorce, sex-obsessed media, and the idolization of youth all send the message that if the relationship gets tough, we should just get out. But the couples with lasting, loving relationships are the ones who hang in there, fighting through problems by talking about them.

In this way, problems actually become opportunities for both mates to learn more about themselves. The greater the problem, the greater the learning that can take place. Like all situations in life, marriage is a continuing process of growth. A marital problem is a gift—often one we don't think we want!—that gives us direction and provides us with information about aspects of ourselves that need attention and thought. All personal growth happens through the confrontation of barriers.

> ***There is a love like a small lamp, which goes out when the oil is consumed; or like a stream which dries up when it doesn't rain. But there is a love that is like a mighty spring gushing up out of the earth; it keeps flowing, forever, and is inexhaustible.***
>
> ISAAC OF SYRIA

Our continuing talk—our communication—keeps us from making assumptions about the thoughts and feelings of our partners, or the meaning of their behavior. Talking allows us to check out our hunches and guesses. We will, of course, give our spouses the same respect we give our friends. We will refrain from using critical or value-laden words and from making statements that attribute blame. Those kinds of words and statements cause others to stop listening and start defending. We will also practice assertiveness, and state our own thoughts and feelings clearly so as to help our partners understand us. And in return, we will listen and try to understand their thoughts and feelings.

> ***Friendships, like marriages, are dependent on avoiding the unforgivable.***
>
> JOHN D. MACDONALD

Only one subject should be taboo in all this talk: the subject of divorce. The mere mention of that word brings it into the realm of possibility. Never forget that words are powerful. If we start using the "D" word in times of anger, soon we'll find it slipping into our more casual discussions. Gradually, we then let divorce become a viable option in our thinking. It becomes tangible, and soon appears inevitable.

> ***Often the difference between a successful marriage and a mediocre one consists of leaving about three or four things a day unsaid.***
>
> HARLAN MILLER

It's natural to want to wrench away from hurt, and when a marriage develops problems, we automatically think about walking out of it. But listening to divorced people, it doesn't sound as if walking out has solved anything. "Our breakup was devastating"; "It's been a year, and I seem to be getting a sense of direction again"; "I feel like running and running, it doesn't matter where, to let the pain, the anger, the destructiveness leave my bones." After divorce, what most people seem to feel is failure—failure that their love wasn't strong or wise or deep enough, or failure at falling for such a "bitch" or "bastard" in the first place, but failure either way. It's a lot to carry. And this is supposed to be a *solution.*

When the temptation to walk out arises, it is our commitment that keeps us resolved to negotiate real solutions to our problems.

If all this sounds a bit too claustrophobic, we must remember that happily married people want the best for each other, which doesn't mean they want to live like Siamese twins, joined in some immutable way. Not all our activities, friends, or enthusiasms will be the same as our mates', and one of the wonderful things about a really strong marriage is that it binds without crippling.

When Dave went back to college for his teaching degree, it meant starting over financially for him and his wife Teresa. But Teresa wanted the best for him, which meant that she wanted him to fulfill his potential. Later, when their child entered school and Teresa decided to become a chef, Dave encouraged her in turn, though again, the decision had repercussions on both their lives. Loving someone doesn't mean that our goals are always identical. Loving means that if we want something, then our mate wants it for us, too.

The great secret of successful marriage is to treat all disasters as incidents and none of the incidents as disasters.

HAROLD NICHOLSON

Love isn't always as glamorous or easy as romance. Love helps us get to the bathroom when we're sick. Love agrees to disagree forever on serious subjects like abortion and gun control. Love is also that moment when we look up and find someone watching us as if we were a candle, as if we were the only light in a world of darkness.

If the notion of lifelong, faithful marriage seems daunting, that's because it is. Yet we must dare to love. Strive for such a goal. And dare it despite knowing that others have similarly dared and lost.

The people people have for friends
Your common sense appall,
But the people people marry
Are the queerest folk of all.

CHARLOTTE GILMAN

AFFIRMATION

I resolve to partake of a deep, monogamous, and ultimate love, bound by willing sacrifice and realized through struggle, courage, and maturity.

TO THINK AND WRITE ABOUT

When your marriage feels sour, who or what is to blame?

If you have a hard time admitting your role in your marital problems, your journal writing will show you how this weakness works in your life. You may find yourself always blaming other people, including your mate, for your personal unhappiness—it is always easier to make someone else accountable.

Working with your journal can also help you overcome the problem. The key is to write your thoughts freely—exactly what happened during an incident. Then, when you later read what you've written, you may be able to see what really took place. Journal writing helps you become increasingly aware of your patterns of thought and behavior.

If you see patterns you'd like to break, you might start to feel a conflict building between your urge to change and the ease of continuing to do what you've always done. As you read your journal entries, you will feel disgusted or offended with yourself and your old habits. That disgust and impatience is exactly what you should feel. It is what will gradually goad you to make course corrections. By becoming aware of your patterns, you'll grow fed up with seeing the same old motifs playing over and over.

Another problem that shows you are avoiding responsibility for your thoughts, emotions, or actions is a lack of the word "I" in your entries.

Understanding and correcting traits that you don't admire in yourself are natural advantages gained through candid writing and subsequent rereading. This system of self-feedback enables you to get a grip on your own life—and your marriage—and to engender the determination to change.

Part Four

Creating a Family

Chapter 7

PARENTHOOD

The Nucleus of Civilization

Before I got married I had six theories about bringing up children; now I have six children and no theories.

JOHN WILMOT, EARL OF ROCHESTER

An undeniable intimacy and mystery characterize human pregnancy. A child will be born, but by what mysterious alchemy? What marvel has changed desire to flesh and started this unique life sprouting like a hidden kernel in the swelling dark of the female body? The Ashanti of West Africa believe that a child's body is formed solely out of the mother's blood. The people of rural Malaysia presume that a child begins in the father's brain. In America, we talk of hormonal cycles, fertility phases, rushing sperm, fusion with an egg that then segments, multiplies, travels, and implants itself in the lining of the uterus. Yet even that doesn't really explain to our satisfaction how life begins. And why do we care so much?

We care because each new life promises that all life will continue, and where there is life there is hope. Even where new generations strain an already congested world, a child is considered a treasure, a demonstration of status, proof of fertility and masculinity, insurance against age and loneliness, a validation of family.

> ***How on earth could he have slaved, denied himself, kept going all those years without the promise for ever before him of the boy's stepping into his shoes carrying on where he left off?***
>
> KATHERINE MANSFIELD

Even where families survive in cellars beneath ravaged buildings, where shells smash, where wells are dry and hands hold empty bowls, birth still holds the finest germ of hope available to us. A child is evidence of the future, evidence that life does not end with this current despair.

In this country, we plan our education, our vacations, our garden rows, and our children. Having a child is another accomplishment to be completed in its proper time. Yet even we can be astounded. We look at our protruding abdomen, and see, feel, the miracle of unborn hope, unborn life. We wonder as we wait—about the baby's sex, size, looks. We worry about its health, about fingers and toes. We also feel uneasy about the coming birth.

> ***With all the pain of it, I long for the wonderful thing to happen, for a tiny human creature to spring from between my limbs bravely out into the world. I need it, just as a true poet needs to create a great undying work.***
>
> YANG PING

Then one day (or night), that wriggling bump in our belly becomes "our daughter," "our son." Pure concept made incarnate.

We bring her home. We sit and look at her, watch her breathe, her facial expressions, the flexing of her limbs. Fascinated, we fall in love. We are dumbfounded, in awe of what we have done.

There follows much conversation about feeding, burping, diaper changes, and baths. The most ordinary things seemed altered, are altered. Everything revolves around the baby. She's a good sound sleeper—or she's not. She has a hardy appetite—or she doesn't. She walks, talks, and becomes potty-trained right on schedule—or doesn't. As the blush of marvel fades, the worries seem larger, because now they are specific: How can we help our baby develop the skills she will need to live in the twenty-first century? How can we help her achieve her full potential? The creation of this new life endows fresh significance to our every action.

> ***Life was diapers and little jars of puréed apricots and bottles and playpens and rectal thermometers, and all those small dirty faces and all those questions.***
>
> PAT LOUD

Though we assume our children won't receive their real education until they enter the first grade, the interval between birth and the age of six is a period of growth and learning unparalleled in later life. Their *real* education? By the time baby skips into first grade, she will have already received it.

What children learn at home, especially in their first years, forms the essential and irreplaceable foundation for everything they learn later. Those first years are crucial in building social underpinnings and intelligence and emotional well-being. It is up to us as parents to help our children become bright, inquisitive, balanced, and pleasurable for others to live with.

> ***I think the most significant work we ever do, in the whole world, in our whole life, is done within the four walls of our own home.***
>
> STEPHEN R. COVEY

The informal education that families so casually give their infant and preschool children makes far more impact on their total education than the entire formal system of schools later on. We are our children's earliest, best, and most important teachers. When we do our job properly, the professionals who come later can provide impressive additional training. If we do not do our job, there isn't much any professional can do. This bleak assessment is the only conclusion possible when we look at the thousands of remedial education programs in existence. Children coming from mediocre environments make mediocre students.

Sensing our tremendous responsibilities, we feel daunted. We feel inadequate. Should we encourage our children to express all their emotions—and perhaps become little tyrants? Should we yell at them—and risk creating a repressed and resentful adults? Neither choice is inviting. Should we spank, or merely give our children the glaring-ats of their lives? Can we teach our nine-month-old baby to swim? Must our three-year-old child be computer literate? Our sense of insecurity makes us listen to whichever "expert" happens to be in the news at the time.

Discipline is a symbol of caring to a child. He needs guidance. . . . A parent must also not be afraid to hang himself. If you have never been hated by your child, you have never been a parent.

BETTE DAVIS

Most of us begin parenting with no knowledge of child development. Because of our culture, we probably haven't even been involved with children since our own childhood. We don't really remember what children are like, and we tread the path of parenthood without any information about the landscape. How do we know when we are at least heading in the right direction, especially when we're bombarded by opposing arguments?

One thing we don't need is more rules. What we do need is a new way of seeing and understanding human beings, a way that takes in the physical, emotional, mental, and spiritual dimensions of what it is to be human. At this point in time, our society prizes children's intellectual development above all else, and tends to ignore other facets of development. Since the launching of *Sputnik* in 1957, in an attempt to produce more intellectual, literate children, we have prodded our elementary-school curriculums to become academic earlier and earlier, so that today kindergartners are taught what was once taught in first grade. It all seems so modern, so neat in theory: Teach them earlier so they can learn more. But it is a theory that forgets that children have a timetable of development as well as an entirely different consciousness from adults. We haven't learned our mistake yet, though many children now fail kindergarten! The only answer "the experts" offer is to goad teachers to start "reading readiness" with four-year-olds.

Children's playings are not sports and should be deemed as their most serious actions.

MONTAIGNE

The experts who encourage early academics, and the parents who blindly follow their advice, are hot-housing preschoolers into scholastic channels—children who should not even be at school, who should be doing the important work of childhood: playing.

In such ways we have let ourselves be convinced that we can engineer our children's maturation. We are encouraged to suspect our natural processes in favor of scientific progress. We want to "do something" rather than allow for our children's own inner unfolding. In Vedic science, the ancient philosophy of India, is a principle called the *economy of effort,* or "do less and achieve more." Western pediatricians reassure parents that each child has a personal schedule. It is our job to reassure ourselves and maintain the self-esteem of our children, who in general terms aren't naturally reading-ready until the age of nine.

A boy may be a brilliant mathematician . . . at the age of thirteen. But I never knew a child of that age who had much that was useful to say about the ends of human life.

ROBERT MAYNARD HUTCHINS

We need to educate ourselves for parenthood enough to recognize the natural timetable of our own children's development. And we should be familiar with children in general. To that end, prospective parents can make friends with experienced parents who can help us remember what children are like. We also need to reconsider our suspicion of nature and the propaganda that encourages us to try to control everything with our minds. Control is an announcement that we don't trust. As wonderful as scientific knowledge may be, it sometimes lulls us into ignoring our own inmost voice of guidance. This renders us unable trust our own intuition.

It is fitting that we question everything, and we should be willing to dig into the deep, rich compost of our experience. From there we can go on to create solutions that feel whole and nourishing, solutions that seek a balance between body, intellect, and spirit.

The solutions will often prove elusive, and that is hard to accept, but being in a condition of "not knowing," of "questioning," is positive even if it feels frustrating. Part of the frustration stems from the fact that our offspring will not wait until we figure it all out. They won't wait until we get more insight and focus. They require constant interaction now. Children don't wait until we are perfect parents. Indeed, we'd better give up the idea of being perfect and instead consider parenting a process in which we can only hope to mature at the same rate our children will. Parents and children may mature on different levels, to be sure, but inevitably we both grow.

Who of us is mature enough for offspring before the offspring themselves arrive? The value of marriage is not that adults produce children but that children produce adults. PETER DE VRIES

Since we can't rely on experts to tell us how to parent, we need to heed our own inner knowing. It's our job to get in touch with ourselves and make our own choices. And we shouldn't expect to be perfect or berate ourselves for mistakes. Our task as parents is not to be gods, but solely to be human beings. Though we may not make the decision to have children in order to provide ourselves with new opportunities to grow, that is exactly what we get. Therefore, we must honor our process as much as we honor our children's.

If we should make the best of this opportunity to grow *with* our children, parenting can help our unfolding as much as we help our children with theirs.

Thou pretty opening rose!
(Go to your mother, child, and wipe your nose!)
Balmy and breathing music like the South,
(He really brings my heart into my mouth!)
Fresh as the morn, and brilliant as its star,
(I wish that window had an iron bar!)
Bold as the hawk, yet gentle as the dove,
(I'll tell you what my love,
I cannot write, unless he's sent above!)

THOMAS HOOD

AFFIRMATION

In parenting my children, I will apply both reason and an open heart—and a willingness to see the possibilities for my own growth.

TO THINK AND WRITE ABOUT

Free association is a classic method of self-discovery. Begin by writing whatever concerns you, such as how you feel about being a parent, or how you feel about getting pregnant. Then simply allow yourself to write down any words, phrases, or sentences that well up. Keep going until the talk in your head dies down to a listening silence.

Reflect on what you've written. Are there contradictions? What else is there?

Much of what you have written will prove unworthy of further consideration. Simply release it as miscellaneous flotsam. But do consider what seems important to you. Don't let feelings of guilt arise if you've written some phrases that would sting or seem unloving if you were to share your writing with anyone else. Release self-judgment so that you can create greater access to the insight of your body and your mind. Remember, what you have written represents your state of being only at the moment that you wrote it. Don't take it too seriously. But recognize that it can help you identify what is floating around between your ears—and in your heart.

Such exercises as this make the difference between living with awareness and stumbling through life at a superficial level. If you do have some negative thoughts about parenting, be glad that you've got them out where you can deal with them. Such loose-drifting negativity can hinder the occurrence of real wisdom.

Chapter 8

INTRODUCING TEENAGERS TO ADULTHOOD

Young Blood Must Have Its Course

> ***Before my daughter was born, I was tempted by the overall cynicism of our age. But when you know that your children and your children's children will be here after you, you suddenly realize that you have a very real responsibility to future generations.***
>
> MARIANNE MOORE

As the dependence of early childhood ebbs, the turbulence of adolescence replaces it. Together with an ever-enlarging competence and independence, our children grow into the necessity to define their identity and determine their way in the world.

The teenage years can be turbulent for both child and parent. Surviving our children's adolescence means accepting the inevitable: Our popularity may go down; our teens' growth spurts and hormonal surges will bewilder both of us; and our once-companionable children will suddenly become privacy freaks.

I think what is happening to me is so wonderful, and not only what can be seen on my body, but all that is taking place inside. I never discuss myself or any of these things with anybody; that is why I have to talk to myself about them. ANNE FRANK

Parents don't have to let this time run through their fingers. We often miss one of the most valuable opportunities of living with teenagers, the possibilities afforded by their natural idealism. Through this, we can show them that we are not as dumb as they feared, continue to nurture their growth, and even help them check their own tendency toward rebellious behavior.

Oh, what a tangled web parents do weave
When they think that their children are naïve.

OGDEN NASH

The rebellion that is also a natural part of adolescence mustn't be stifled completely. It will appear in some form regardless. The teenager of very strict parents who demand monthly haircuts and polite speech *will* come home wearing pink shoes. That might seem like a relatively harmless rebellion to permissive parents who have never interfered with their teenager's grooming. Their teen, however, may come home with a tattoo. Teenagers simply must step over the line, wherever we draw it. We should expect it and not feel as if we've failed when it happens.

As a child, you are brought up in a world of discipline, of obedience, and you are dependent on

others. All this has to be transcended as you come to maturity. JOSEPH CAMPBELL

Adolescents are not irritable or uncooperative or rebellious because they want to hurt us. They are testing themselves and the world, and they are doing so within the safety of their family. Looked at from that viewpoint, it is actually a compliment that we have given them a place in which they feel safe enough to vent their volcanoes. Of course, it is our obligation as parents to see that they don't burn themselves.

We shouldn't try to avoid conflicts with our teens altogether. Strangely, that would be a form of neglect. It is our job to teach our teens the self-discipline that is necessary for their ultimate independence from us. When we avoid struggles with them, we don't allow them to develop their true strength. Slow, slogging effort is the only route to authentic maturity of mind and emotion, and we shouldn't hand over control of their lives before they have found that maturity. We can't abandon them to their own meager devices too soon.

Drama is the stuff of adolescent life. Teenagers arrested for vandalism and robbery often have no motivation except the excitement of stealing a car or breaking into a school. Though such extreme rebellion should not be ignored, it is a mistake for us to allow ourselves to become emotionally triggered whenever our teens act like teens. We certainly don't want to establish a pattern in which our children get their daily "hit" of drama from interacting with *us*.

Young men, in the conduct and manage of actions, embrace more than they can hold; stir more than they can quiet; fly to the end without consideration of the means and degrees. FRANCIS BACON

Which isn't to say that we should give up legitimate rules and expectations in the face of a teenager's withering opinions. Almost half of all teens today say they don't have enough freedom—in this, the most liberal age of all time! As parents, we should be willing to reexamine our standards to see if they are reasonable, and then we should hold fast to those rules we believe are good for our teenagers and for our families in general. Such things as curfews and being informed about their whereabouts at all times are vital.

Teens and Drinking: Most called drinking a serious problem; 22% said they drank regularly.

1994 *USA WEEKEND* POLL

Nor should we let our kids absent themselves from family dinners, visits to relatives, vacations, and other "boring" rituals. Whether they know it or not, they need a continuing sense of being part of families that value them. Even if they just sit in a corner and behave in the most jaded manner, they feel more secure knowing that their families are still families and that they have central places in them.

Adolescence is the period of the decisive last battle fought before maturity. The ego must achieve independence, the old emotional ties must be cast off, and new ones created.

HELENE DEUTSCH

Teens will lobby against every rule, but if we actually did give up our essential standards, they would feel abandoned and unloved. We shouldn't abdicate our high expectations, especially in matters of appropriate social behavior and responsible citizenship.

Teenagers would be surprised to know that their rejection of us often hurts. We love them, and we miss the more companionable friendship we had with them when they were younger. But there is no point in pursuing adolescents who are reluctant to be open with us. We have the right to expect basic information about where they are and what they're doing, but we cannot make them share what they are feeling or thinking. However, inquiring respectfully about their thoughts and feelings is admissible, as long as we accept what they give us without pushing for more, and without trying to make them see that they're wrong and we're right. This is the time to work out the kinks in the adult-to-adult relationship with them that we hope to continue the rest of our lives. We must not ask for more of them than adult friends ask of one another.

Now is the time to create new rituals. It might be shopping together, going to ball games, learning to play chess together, or meeting for a weekly luncheon date. And when treated respectfully, once in a while our teenagers will actually want to talk to us.

Not always at a time we have planned for, of course, but when they choose.

To teach is to learn. JAPANESE PROVERB

The talks that teens most enjoy are discussions of "ideals." Adolescence is the most idealistic of all the stages humans grow through. Indeed, our teens can reinspire us if we give them a chance. In turn, we can introduce facts they haven't considered yet. This takes a light hand, of course, and if these conversations are to be enjoyed, we must not "tell" our children what is so and what is not so. If these talks are to be continued at regular intervals, we must go into them with an attitude of permitting our children to explore various ideas and hold various opinions, even if we're certain they're wrong. (We mustn't forget, the ways to truth converge from many directions.) Fear of new or variant ideas is death to intellectual growth, and fear of expressing variant ideas is death to parent-child relationships. Adolescents are capable of far more than adults often assume. We must trust that they will work through some of their wilder notions and eventually settle on the bedrock of logic and truth.

> ***To grown people a girl of fifteen and a half is a child still; to herself she is very old and very real; more real, perhaps, than ever before or after.***
>
> MARGARET WIDDEMER

We can also make ourselves available when our children entertain their friends in our homes. Often their friends, who have no agenda with us, will be happy to enter discussions with us, and will even treat our insights with respect. This validates us to our own children, who value the opinions of their peers above everything just now. There is no higher accolade than for our teens to tell us that their friends like us.

(But, please, let's not try to "be one of the gang." Our involvement with our children's friends should be appropriate, invited, and well-spaced.)

By taking advantage of this developmental stage of idealism, parents are usually surprised that the teen years, while still challenging, can be much more constructive than they expected. Being the parents of teenagers may not be the best thing that ever happens to us, but it can be rewarding, positive, and special. And it can continue our own growth by requiring something different of us as parents. The key is to squelch our negative assumptions and let our excitement about the untapped potential of our blossoming young people prevail—a potential that involves nothing less than their intellectual, moral, physical, emotional, and social development.

> ***Growing is not the easy, plain sailing business that it is commonly supposed to be: it is hard work, harder than any but a growing boy can understand.***
> SAMUEL BUTLER

Teenagers are in transition from concrete to abstract thinking. They are intensely curious and have a wide-open attitude about intellectual pursuits. They would rather learn by doing than by listening to lectures. Unfortunately, this is exactly when high schools subject them to the lecture system of education. To keep their interest in preparing for their futures alive, we parents can provide much of the immediate experiences that make what they're learning in high school relevant. We can arrange vacations that take in art galleries and hands-on science museums. If we live in small towns, we can visit cities with our teens; if we live in cities, we can take them into rural settings. We can show them the world—and plant seeds as we go about how they might consider rooting in it themselves when their time comes.

One way in which adolescent idealism is especially wonderful is in its budding consideration for the rights of others. Teens often show compassion for animals, the downtrodden, and the environment. The way their brains are maturing at this point serves well for sinking their teeth into morally active subjects like world peace, ecology, and racism. Now might be the time to introduce volunteerism to them.

I hear and I forget. I see and I remember. I do and I understand. CHINESE PROVERB

A more difficult aspect of this stage is that teens often forget all we've taught them about self-esteem. They are growing so fast that sometimes they're surprised at the length of their own legs and arms. Suddenly they are as uncoordinated and accident-prone as a toddler. The little girl now becomes tall, ungainly, long-waisted, and long-legged—while the little boy may remain little, with a wild cowlick and big ears. They mature at different rates, and we find knobby knees and baby faces in the same group as curvaceous bodies and beards. Hormones cause both restlessness and fatigue. Good nutrition is critical at this final stage of growth, but they prefer chips and soda—or they may shun food in an effort to look like the models they see in magazines.

He didn't play with his food anymore till it got cold; instead, down it went like fuel into a furnace keeping the ovens hot, and the energy at boiling point, as Tom hurtled through his life catching up with himself at last. SHELAGH DELANEY

Intense and unpredictable mood swings are also normal. Their need to release tension sometimes results in sudden, apparently meaningless outbursts. Being accepted by peers is a top priority, but parents can do nothing right—we give them too much attention, too little attention; we drive too slowly, too fast; we dress too young for our age, or we act like old fogies.

They are just as critical of themselves and compare themselves not only with their peers, but also with super athletes and movie stars. This is no time for us to stop stressing the need to love oneself and the value of being unique.

In a sense, these are our last-chance years. This is our last chance, as parents, to nurture our kids so they grow up with self-esteem and resilience.

But they are on the road to separation, and we frankly don't have as much influence. Peer pressure is natural. It comes with our teenagers' awareness of the world at large, into which they must soon travel—without us. We all have a deep, fundamental human longing to belong. In teenagers, this manifests as a strong need to belong to a group. They experiment with new slang and new behaviors, even copycat behaviors. Their schoolwork may suffer because the social world is so compelling. Their sexual hormones are clamoring. They experience intense desires. They also experience intense love—and real heartbreak. Though they may not have the maturity or the skills to handle these adult emotions, their feelings are just as real and should be given consideration.

> ***Sensuality is burgeoning. . . . I feel at once grave, ill at ease and happy as I watch our children—our*** **children**—***growing to meet the greatest of instincts. May it have mercy on them!*** — KÄTHE KILLWITZ

As parents, our personal assignment is to practice becoming coaches, mentors, and adult friends to our developing children. We must prepare ourselves for the smaller position we will inevitably hold in their lives. This may bring us some sadness, but nature provides the antidote: To see our children growing into complete people ready to take on the world is one of the most gratifying things life has to offer.

Don't laugh at a youth for his affectations, he's only trying on one face after another till he finds his own. LOGAN PEARSALL SMITH

AFFIRMATION

I will get in touch with my own idealism in order to maintain a gate through the wall that my teenager tries to build between us.

TO THINK AND WRITE ABOUT

Let yourself return to adolescence in your journal, at least insofar as you allow your spontaneous, creative self to lead the way. Relax, give yourself permission to experiment, take chances. Write yourself into a tangled knot of barbed wire now and then. It's all right. Quiet your internal critic—or let it speak freely, revealing all its priggish opinions. Hear its voice and write out everything it has to say. Then be sure to answer it. Argue with it until it gives you permission to continue with your own growth toward maturity.

Part Five

Life's Work

Chapter 9

Harnessing Our Ambition

Build Thee More Stately Mansions, O My Soul

We have a basic drive for growth and mastery that is expressed in a variety of specific ambitions. This is a universal characteristic of humans, shared equally by men and women, varying little in history or across different cultures. GILBERT BRIM

Studies show that chimpanzees and apes will perform almost any task just to be allowed to play with a new object introduced to their surroundings. Rats show the same curiosity and desire to explore. Human beings also want to be challenged, and this simple truth stands behind all our ambitions.

We are a purposeful species. Many of our thoughts are about intentions, plans, wishes, hopes, and beliefs. Furthermore, we create strategies of action to get what we want. We are left dissatisfied by whatever accomplishments or knowledge we already have; we crave new achievements—occasions to experiment with and try out new abilities. Young or old, we want to be challenged, to shape, form, and build our own lives. One of the most vivid events for parents is to hear their child shout, "Me do it!"

> ***I hold it truth, with him who sings***
> ***To one clear hope in divers tones,***
> ***That men may rise on stepping stones***
> ***Of their dead selves to higher things.***
>
> LORD TENNYSON

Studies of job satisfaction give convincing evidence that challenge and autonomy make work more satisfying to adults. Some of us tolerate dull jobs by directing our urge for growth and mastery toward other goals. For example, Benedict Spinoza, the seventeenth-century Dutch philosopher, ground lenses while creating his ideology. The nineteenth-century philosopher John Stuart Mill did correspondence for the East India Company and, on the side, wrote major works on economic and political theory. And early in this century, Albert Einstein examined patent applications as he formed his theories of the universe. Most of us are not so illustrious, but when we cannot find what we need in our work, we too search elsewhere. By improving our bowling, mastering a six-iron shot on a downhill lie, or making the perfect omelet, we satisfy our ambitions.

Psychologists who study aging find that growth and mastery are central even to elderly people's sense of well-being. The urge to grow continues throughout life.

> ***What answer to the meaning of existence should one require beyond the right to exercise one's gifts?***
>
> W. H. AUDEN

Surgeons, poets, and obsessed geniuses receive callings that impose legitimate goals. Indeed, they often cannot ignore the lure of their vocations. But the rest of us also have ambitions, though perhaps not so lofty. We are, as a species and as individuals, thoroughly ambitious. We want . . . oh, we want so very many things, and we want them all so much! We may not know the purpose of our lives, but we can conclude that this natural ambition must be the engine of some appointment with destiny.

However, when we don't understand the urges at work in us, we may act out ambitions that we don't know about. Or we may move from temporary goal to temporary goal. As a door opens, we slip through it, and in that room we look for another door. We see only the walls that enclose us, and it isn't clear until we see the next door opening that something else is possible.

Some of us do plan for the longer term. We have images of where we expect to be and what we expect to be doing at specific times in our future. Granted, these visions may be fuzzy. They may never come true. Nevertheless, we have a life plan of sorts.

> ***I have learned this at least by my experiment: that if one advances confidently in the direction of his dreams, and endeavors to live the life which he has imagined, he will meet with success unexpected in common hours.***
>
> HENRY DAVID THOREAU

A purposeful life has three elements: desired goals; a timetable for how long it will take to achieve them; and the behavior, or means, for achieving them. It seems quite simple, doesn't it?

But our ambitions are mixed up with our personalities and with all the natural purities and impurities of the world, among them envy, greed, and insatiability. Just as we are not exemplary, our ambitions are not either, and mixed in with our hunger for excellence and commitment there may be hunger for things much less admirable.

> ***When you're ambitious, it's really hard to be supportive of other people. But I think it's our job to try, even though one gets jealous.***
>
> SQUEAK CARNWATH

We can feel deep disappointment if someone else achieves "our" goal. Or, aspiring to reach the snow-slicked mountaintop, we can forget to love the plain earth right under our feet. Ambition is vital, but it can be damaging or even dangerous. It is a keen and driving force, but we need to know exactly what edges it can drive us over.

> ***Glories, like glow-wormes, afarre off shine bright,***
> ***But lookt to neare, have neither heat nor light.***
>
> JOHN WEBSTER

When we make up our lives as we go along, we don't always get them right. How do we figure out what to do from one day to the next? It's painful to be without direction. There are considerable arguments for planning ahead. We all want a life we love, a good life. Someone described a good life as one in which we get up in the morning eager to start each new day. Having a goal can help. Life is too short to live without focus. Studies reveal that people who call themselves happy know exactly what they want and feel they are moving toward getting it. Life feels good when it has direction, when we are headed toward what we want.

The first hurdle for many of us, though, is to figure out what that is. Our goals have to have meaning for us. We can't just take the path of least resistance. Nor can we look to others for our goals. Too often, we let others decide what is expected of us. We may never say it out loud, but we are often worried about what "they" will think. The expectations of others have a powerful effect on how we run our lives.

> ***Now, however, I see the folly of attempting to hitch one's wagon to a star with a harness that does not belong to it.***
> HELEN KELLER

We're reared in families and cultures that barrage us with messages about what others want from us. These messages, supple as shadows, stay inside us and may remain unexamined throughout our lives, undermining our happiness in several ways. If we do something other than what society expects of us, even if it fascinates us and makes us thrive, we have a nagging feeling that we're not doing what we're *supposed* to be doing. For instance, what if the message inside us says in a schoolteachery voice that we're supposed to *marry* a successful person, not *be* one? First, our own success is robbed of its satisfaction, and second, we feel a failure for succeeding in the way we weren't "supposed to." It's easy to see how hurtful some supposed-to messages can be. Many of us feel we have no right to our own brand of joy, our own ambitions. For these reasons, we must take a careful look at what the other people in our lives want from us.

If we don't congratulate and celebrate ourselves, we must look elsewhere for validation. This makes us more dependent on others for recognition and approval. SUSAN SCHENKEL

Next, we need to look for what it is that *we* want. The clues often lie in our dissatisfactions. Inside every discontent is an unsatisfied want. Whenever we're experiencing a negative emotion, we should ask ourselves, "What do I want?"

It may seem easier to do what is expected of us and live with the vague sense that something is missing. If we do decide to live our own lives, however, we must be patient with ourselves. Even when we decide to change, our automatic responses will for a long time lag behind. It helps to be around others who are also in the process of exploring their habits.

I have always been driven by some distant music—a battle hymn no doubt—for I have been at war from the beginning. BETTE DAVIS

Discovering the right goals for us is like waking up to who we are. The goals themselves feel powerful, impelling, because they have the full force of the self emerging from bondage. Expressing these desires brings a distinct response we can't miss: We *know* we can achieve them. We can literally see, smell, and taste our success. There is no need to force our minds to concentrate on something we deeply want and feel we deserve. Our inner response tells us that our goal is on target.

Becoming prosperous is first of all being truthful to ourselves. RUTH ROSS

Knowing what we want in life is a reward in itself. It gives us the excitement and energy we need to make our wanting deliberate. Our next task is to be specific about our plans. We do that by focusing on the details of our ambition. Focusing intensifies energy in the same way a magnifying glass held over kindling intensifies the sun's power. The more specific we are about our goals, the more conscious we become about reaching them.

Somebody said that it couldn't be done,
But he with a chuckle replied
That "maybe it couldn't," but he would be one,
who wouldn't say so till he'd tried.

EDGAR A. GUEST

Without planning, there is no reliable method of achieving our ambitions. We need to establish a strategy. We can do this by writing a specific goal, or goals, we want to achieve in five years.

The man who was not content to do small things well would leave great things undone.

ELLEN GLASGOW

How do we want to be living five years from now? Of course, the future is beyond our control; we need to leave room for uncertainty. But we also need an attitude of confidence. So, what needs to happen in four years in order for us to reach that five-year place? In three years? Two years? In this backwards manner, we come to our goals for the next year. Then, what must we do next month? Next week? This week?

This is where we may lean back in a bone-popping stretch, as our attempts at goal-making face their first test: Do we really intend to do what is necessary this month, and this week? We can't get from point A to point B without accomplishing point A. If we know we can't achieve the steps as quickly as our plan suggests, we should revamp the entire schedule. Maybe it will take us ten years instead of five to reach point B—but we'll never reach it if we don't make a plan that we can realistically follow.

Dreams grow holy put in action.

ADELAIDE PROCTOR

Next, we establish a pattern of starting each day by reviewing our weekly goals and deciding what we can do today toward achieving them. In this way, we keep our minds focused on where we are heading. Still, it's easier to get our minds stirred up to a froth than to actually take the action needed. But action is essential. Luck is nice, but the amount of good luck that comes our way depends on our own willingness to act. Action not only helps us move ahead, it helps us clarify our thoughts. Even action in the wrong direction is informative. By exposing ourselves to real-life experiences and seeing how they feel, action helps us make necessary course corrections.

Think like a man of action, act like a man of thought.

HENRI BERGSON

Action also raises our self-esteem. Most inaction is due to fear. Every time we do something a little scary, our self-esteem goes up a degree. Confidence spreads from things we do successfully to a general feeling that we can learn to do other things.

Also, opportunity (luck?) pops up once we're in action.

Another important result of action is less tangible: As a stream shapes its embankments, through doing what we want to become, we become what we do.

So we must take action. But what if we do find our goals were not quite on target? Well, we change them and again take action. We decide to be. We decide to make it happen. Our goals will change as we change. Goal-planning has no respite. Each of us really is the master of his or her own fate. And we must be willing to take some risks.

> ***The purpose of life is a life of purpose.***
>
> ROBERT BYRNE

Our internal reference point remains our own ambitions. We have to continually resist seeking the approval of others. We must stop thinking and behaving in anticipation of "their" response. That, too, is scary. But the most successful people in the world are just as fearful as we are. Leaving the familiar is universally frightening, sometimes even painful. The only difference between those who are successful and those who aren't is that the successful people just keep putting one foot in front of the other, in spite of their fears.

> ***I do want to get rich but I never want to do what there is to do to get rich.***
>
> GERTRUDE STEIN

Much of the art of living depends on this ability to decide what we want and then to arrange our lives to make it happen.

Harnessing our natural ambition may mean making unpopular decisions sometimes. It may mean making sacrifices to bring about the changes that ultimately make us happier. The alternative is to live a muted life, as if in a plastic bubble, always looking out at those who are experiencing the complete sensation of being.

> *Keep away from people who try to belittle your ambitions. Small people always do that, but the really great make you feel that you, too, can become great.*
>
> MARK TWAIN

AFFIRMATION

I will live the life that has been given to me, and let others live the lives that have been given to them.

TO THINK AND WRITE ABOUT

An outline is a collection of related topics and subtopics. Using your journal, try outlining your desired life in this way:

I. My life
  A. Work
  B. Relationships
  C. Home
  D. Recreation
  E. Money

Use whatever topics seem important and appropriate. You may start with some of the topics considered in this book.

Under each, begin a list of subtopics. For instance, under *A. Work* you may list practical things like: *1. A salary of* $X0,000. You may also list more abstract things like: 2. *Meaningful work.*

As you give this outline thought over time, you will no doubt get even more specific, so that under your subtopics you will continue the outline format. Under 2. *Meaningful work,* you may list *a. Use my creativity.*

Forget the rule about needing at least two items at each level. If you only have one item at an *a.* level, so what? This is your outline; you're not making it for "them." Yes, break a rule! Feel your upwelling confidence, your upwelling life.

Studies show that merely writing down your ambitions makes you much more likely to achieve them. Can you afford not to give yourself a head start?

Chapter 10

DEFINING SUCCESS

To Burn Always with This Hard, Gemlike Flame

> ***There is only one success—to be able to spend your life in your own way.***
>
> CHRISTOPHER MORLEY

Perhaps it starts in school, when we study history and memorize the names of kings and queens and presidents. Or later, when we have seen too many *Time* magazine "Man of the Year" covers. However it happens, we tend to see success as monolithic. Successful people appear to have harnessed themselves to the secret tides of history. The very word "success" connotes superior achievement, garnering wealth, power, and celebrity. It means being paid a million dollars to appear in a movie, or making a cool billion in computers. Inevitably we take these super-successes for our models. After all, doesn't the media take pains to show how these people were originally shaped from common clay just like us? But unlike us, they have become "somebodies." How are we supposed to feel when we don't become somebodies, too? Like failures?

If you are born and raised in the boondocks and have the slightest sense of ambition, one fact becomes clear . . . : that out there, away from your little bend on Moon River, people are doing interesting things, having more fun, and in the end, accomplishing things that one cannot undertake locally.

RICHARD SCHICKEL

If success is synonymous with reward, power, and acclaim, then it follows that any kind of merit can be detected by our net worth, the magazine covers to our credit, and the people we can boss around.

Let's talk about these factors separately, beginning with power and its attendant, fame. We most often think of power as domination—not only the ability to order other people around, but to be listened to by journalists and talk-show hosts. The downside of this is that most of us don't really want to be asked if we sleep in the nude. Fame has a contemptuous way of making people look and feel whorish.

This kind of power takes its toll of time, energy, and integrity. And in the end, it limits our choices. Surely, real power should include the power to do what we want with our lives? And shouldn't it be involved in serious matters? Most of the news-makers we read about—the politicians and the people with famous causes—spout ideologies that are in essence irrelevant to almost everyone.

Most of us know we would not be happy with the kind of success portrayed on corner newsstands. We wouldn't want to deal with the problems of such extreme celebrity. We wouldn't want to redefine ourselves in movie star terms. Not many of us really want flashguns popping in our faces. We don't want to be media "products."

Television is to news what bumper stickers are to philosophy. RICHARD M. NIXON

As for riches, there is a peak of satisfaction that can be reached by having money and the things that money can buy. We have a built-in set point called "enough," and accumulating wealth beyond that point actually lessens satisfaction.

Despite this reality-check, the correlation between commercial success and true success grows ever more distant in our value system as the magazine-cover brand of success blunts our capacity to fully conceive our own roles—our own selves—as successful.

Unfortunately in America today, either you're a star or you're nobody. MICHAEL BENNET

There is, in any culture of prominence, an elite, which serves as the repository of the highest intellectual and artistic attainments and the sensor of what is worthy. But with our electronic age, a magnified and multiplied image of elitism is tyrannizing our lives. We need to reimagine success according to what author Kirkpatrick Sale termed a "human scale." Our image of success should owe nothing to the media with its ready-to-wear metaphors. Human possibility, after all, extends far beyond what celebrated faces infer by their presence (and sell with their endorsements). Work of quality proceeds. It cannot be otherwise, given the energy and resources we non-superstars pour into it.

We need a more spiritual approach to success, and fortunately another standard is available, one far more real and attainable. It allows for being our own boss, enlarges our self-esteem, and provides opportunity to develop our personal tastes and styles. Let's call it the Success of Living Well.

You have reached the pinnacle of success as soon as you become uninterested in money, compliments, or publicity. — O. A. BATTISTA

By living well we rekindle our dreams and reclaim our lives. We start putting the pieces together so that what is most important to us comes first. The person who lives well builds her work around her life instead of the other way around. She defines success as earning her living in harmony with her interests, values, and priorities. She creates a life that functions the way she needs and wants it to.

This brand of achievement promotes pursuing and reaching our individual ideals. It calls for a life journey that is a creative process. It allows us to explore many avenues that can take us to our desires, and to choose the most appealing.

To laugh often and much; to win the respect of intelligent people and the affection of children; to earn the appreciation of honest critics and endure the betrayal of false friends; to appreciate beauty, to find the best in others; to leave the world a bit better, whether by a healthy child, a garden patch or a redeemed social condition; to know even one life has breathed easier because you have lived. This is to have succeeded. — RALPH WALDO EMERSON

The process of living well resembles the process of creating a work of art: It may use certain stock sets or pieces, and there may be influence from those who have gone before, but there is also freedom of expression. No well-lived life is a mere copy of someone else's life. The task of living well is very much like creating art. Life and art both call for a balance of freedom and discipline. Both take place in real time. Both demand an ability to bend the lines of tradition in some new, unprecedented shape. And both require inventiveness.

If we approach each day as an artist approaches a blank canvas, neither willing to paint by the numbers nor trying to duplicate some mass-media success, then we confront the challenge of creation. And what we are creating are our own lives.

> ***I believe that our aesthetic sense, whether in works of art or in lives, has overfocused on the stubborn struggle toward a single goal rather than on the fluid, the protean, the improvisatory.***
>
> CATHERINE BATESON

Defining personal images of success is one of our most important tasks. Very early we learn that we are judged on output and productivity and scores. To live well, however, we must figure out what it means to be our best selves. There can be no external measure of that.

Many of us are driven by a need for recognition. Being recognized is easiest if we make a lot of money and spend it extravagantly. Money in this country has always been the number one means of keeping score. But we are capable of creating a new definition of success.

> ***I think I can.***
>
> *THE LITTLE ENGINE THAT COULD*

To do so, we can't settle for what our culture hands us as a measure of success. Although money may seem the embodiment of accomplishment, making more money and gaining more power are simply *not* synonymous with success. They're not even synonymous with happiness. In reality, they often bring a profound sense of disappointment.

Money can take its proper place in our lives only when our *selves* are nourished and satisfied.

> ***We hold these Truths to be self-evident, that all Men are created equal, that they are endowed by their Creator with certain unalienable Rights, that among these are Life, Liberty, and the Pursuit of Happiness.*** DECLARATION OF INDEPENDENCE

It is completely up to each one of us to invent our own success framework for living well. In many ways, accepting the given standards frees us from experiencing any angst about what to do. In fact, just stepping out from under that umbrella is hair-raising for many of us. We're suddenly confronted with the problem of freedom and what to do with it. Many of us would rather escape that particular responsibility. In doing so, we shackle ourselves to a set of standards and rules that prohibit us from leading truly successful lives—well-lived lives.

Success at living well suggests attaining a sense of comfort and deep enjoyment. It infers that what is of most importance to us is not relegated to the fringes and hollows of our days. It also suggests that we live in accordance with our values.

> ***Millions long for immortality who do not know what to do with themselves on a rainy Sunday afternoon.*** SUSAN ERTZ

Measure our success by the joy and comfort we experience in our lives? Is it really that easy? Yes, and that hard, too. It means working toward a success that is meaningful to us.

Let's look at an example. Sean was brought up on both football and camping. He had athletic talent, and his goal was to be a superstar player. In college, he studied forest management—and football. He excelled in his classes, yet also did well enough on the playing field to be drafted. As a pro he was not on the starting lineup, though he played often. His parents were proud of him, and others saw him as successful, but he felt no satisfaction at all.

Identifying and accepting our success can be almost as difficult as achieving it. Some of us, like Sean, have a very hard time believing we are "there." We can't accept it, or "it" is suddenly not enough.

Paradoxically, those who tend to do this are the very ones who are most desperate to know they're competent. This is a self-esteem issue of a unique type. Unique, because often we know we're able and that we have done well—but that isn't enough. We feel we must be brilliant, outstanding, even geniuses. We are truly victims of the Great Success myth. Anything *we're* able to accomplish must not be very important or difficult. Even when we've obviously done well, we can only think of our failings. We're painfully aware of how we could still improve.

In Sean's case, he couldn't see his success. He only saw that he was not on the starting lineup.

The real demon is success—the anxieties engendered by this quest are relentless, degrading, corroding. What is worse, there is no end to this escalation of desire. MARGARET FISHBACK

The fact that others are able to do well, too, seems proof that we can't possibly feel satisfied with our achievements. If we're not "special," we haven't succeeded. The Great Success myth breeds a need to be perfect and prevents us from enjoying what we do accomplish. Sometimes it even prevents us from reaching higher goals. What if we failed?

If we each have to become stars before we can feel worthwhile, we are seldom going to be satisfied. Further, we're going to feel an overall dissatisfaction with our lives. Using that unrealistic gauge, our work is never going to be as good or original as it should be. It could always be better. We dismiss our real talents and presume we are mediocre if we're not *the very best.*

Our sense of self-esteem and our self-confidence have a great impact on our enjoyment of our success. Even if we should happen to feel successful now and then, we aren't able to truly let ourselves feel confident about our ability to continue succeeding. We feel hopeless and helpless, and we think, "No matter what I do, it's not enough. I can never really be successful."

> ***There are surely lives which display very few of the signs of success, until very late, or after life is over. There are lives of great significance which go unrecognized by peers for a very long time, there are those who achieve nothing for themselves but leave a legacy for others who come after, there are lives sacrificed for causes.*** SONYA RUDIKOFF

The Great Success myth causes us to take our real successes for granted while exerting great pressure on us to be outstanding, special, the very best. It breeds perfectionist and critical standards. The sad thing is that it prevents us from ever knowing our own success; it puts us on a treadmill, where no matter how fast we go or how long we run we never seem to reach the elusive goal.

Success in life could be defined as the continued expansion of happiness and the progressive realization of worthy goals. DEEPAK CHOPRA

Sean, our football pro, learned the folly of the Great Success myth in time to turn his life around. He realized he didn't have to be the best football player of all time. In fact, the game began to bore him. He gave it up and became a forest ranger. He made about one-third the money, but the work was three times more personally satisfying. By stepping out of the Great Success game, his days began to have meaning again. He had reason to greet each morning. His work gave him new energy.

"I see guys I used to play with, and they're envious—not of my salary, of course, but of the sense of purpose I get from what I'm doing."

An added benefit of working in the peace of the outdoors was that Sean's cornucopia of thoughts filled until it overflowed. He began to write poetry, using a uniquely rich and ruddy language. He found an entire new area of interest—which he may never have discovered if he'd continued to plow all his energies into striving for superstardom.

No trumpets sound when the important decisions of our lives are made. AGNES DE MILLE

We don't have to be Great Successes. We can be successful being ourselves. We only have to be *good,* not the best. If we can learn this, our chances of success will be greater than ever. Certainly our enjoyment of it will be. If we don't learn this, we are doomed to constant dissatisfaction with ourselves, our jobs, and those around us. And our own lives will be far less impressive than they could have been.

We have to learn how to remain unimpressed by splashy Hollywood and Washington, DC, success imagery. The new representation in our heads must be more eloquent than that, more thoughtful, and more satisfying.

> ***The merely egotistical satisfactions of fame are easily nullified by a toothache.*** GEORGE ELIOT

AFFIRMATION

I will resist feeling diminished by media images of success, and confidently hold up my own measurement based on my own values.

TO THINK AND WRITE ABOUT

Even the most average life has a deep underground river of inner significance. You can access your river through autobiographical writing. It can help you see the meaning and continuity in your life, tie together the loose ends, and lead you to a sense of personal conclusion. If the idea of writing your own life story intimidates you, you will be glad to know there are many guides available. The easiest offer a simple question format, which you answer in as much detail as you choose. Questions are arranged in a logical order, beginning with

"Where were you born?" and continuing chronologically to help you organize your lifetime of experiences. It's important to include how you felt about the events of your life and what you thought about them.

You don't have to write your story all at once. You can work at it over weeks—or years. Separate part of your journal just for your story, or put your autobiographical writing right in with your dated entries.

In a very natural way, reviewing your life will help you find points of meaning, which in turn will help you judge your success.

PART SIX

LIFE AFTER WORK

Chapter 11

Having It All

The Hidden Soul of Harmony

Balance is not achieved by succumbing to great highs and horrible lows, wild fluctuations in mood and mind, terrible drinking bouts, rages and madnesses, and then surviving to tell the tale. Rather, balance is steadfastness in the face of inner and outer turmoil. It is both delicacy and resoluteness, it is the passionate moderation of passion.

ERIC MAISEL

The women's liberation movement of the 1970s brought to light not only assertiveness but another term, "having it all." For women, it meant being able to marry *and* have a family *and* work at meaningful employment. Today, it is used by both men and women, and it infers having satisfying work, family hours, leisure pursuits, friendships, travel, continuing education, and spiritual growth.

A lot to ask of one lifetime. But considering our technological and mechanical civilization, we should be able to manage well. So why aren't we?

Modern life is full of conveniences that previous generations would have found mind-boggling. We live in a world that would sound like pure science fiction—or a tall tale—to past eras. Conrad Richter's excellent novel, *The Trees,* portrays the lives of a family living in the United States just two hundred years ago. The men hunted tirelessly to provide food. Before the women could cook it, a tree had to be chopped down, the wood split into fire lengths. After the family ate, their wooden dishes had to be washed. They tanned the animal's skin, and cut and sewed it for clothing. The men trekked through dense, pathless woods to the nearest trading post to barter any extra skins for coarsely ground cornmeal, which they carried home on their backs. That yellow meal was mixed and baked in the ashes of a fire before it could be eaten as bread. The children fished, trapped, carried water, and gathered nuts and berries.

Happiness is a way-station between too little and too much. CHANNING POLLOCK

In past eras, food, clothing, and shelter were the daily concerns of every man, woman, and child. The necessities of life took all their strength and consideration, day in and day out.

Today, we stop off at the store after work to pick up some bread and meat. We carry it home in our cars, and if any cooking has to be done, we use microwaves and temperature-controlled ovens. The soiled dishes we pack into an automatic washer. Our closets are full of clothing we've purchased off laden racks. The most difficult aspect of providing for our basic needs is perhaps searching out a good sale.

We live on a plane of convenience and security miles above that of our forebears, yet we feel harried and hurried and tired. Why? Why doesn't having it all feel as good as it sounds?

She had to live not in that passing world but in her own deeps. PEARL S. BUCK

In ancient Greece, it was considered tawdry to work. Slaves worked so that the elite could pursue the finer things in life. Today, our work-saving technology provides each of us with the equivalent of several personal slaves. It should free us to pursue those finer things the Greeks cared about, but instead, statistics tell us that we're working more hours than our parents did. What's going on?

Lazy, bone-lazy, they wish to believe that life is lived simply by living. REBECCA WEST

For one thing, we're not content to live at the level that even the Greek elite considered fitting, let alone backwoods pioneers. When we say we want to have it all, we really mean we want to *own* it all, *do* it all, *see* it all, and *know* it all. And this creates a lot of demand on our time, relationships, and nervous systems. Because we have so many desires tugging at our hems, it becomes hard to balance our attention. Because there are so many things available, it becomes hard to balance our resources and desires. Because we have so many options, choices, and opportunities, it becomes hard to weigh our priorities. Because we have so many possessions and obligations, it becomes hard to balance our time.

I must find a way to live more simply.

RUTH ST. DENIS

We have the same energy and the same hours per day as people of former generations, but we have many more desires. And many more things. There's a lot of traffic in our lives, and unfortunately, the busier it is, the emptier life becomes.

We live in the first period and place in the world's history where challenges stem not from scarcity but from surplus, not from oppression but from opportunities, and not from absence but from abundance. Instead of struggling to gather our next meal, we struggle to gather our families together long enough to eat one. Rather than fighting a foreign government (or a slave master) in order to make our own decisions, we are reeling from hundreds of TV channels, thousands of consumer items, and unlimited educational, employment, and lifestyle alternatives.

It isn't the sparse simplicity of shortage but the crowded complications of profusion that plague us, and our salvation lies not in the balance of our abilities but in our ability to balance.

> ***When we depend less on industrially produced consumer goods, we can live in quiet places. Our bodies become vigorous; we discover the serenity of living with the rhythms of the earth. We cease oppressing one another.*** ALICIA BAY LAUREL

When the juggler at the street fair loses his concentration, misses a ball, and then grabs for the others as they fall, we are embarrassed for him. In life, the imbalance is harder to see. We hide our stress and frustration. We conceal our worry that things are wrong in our families and that we're neglecting important things—like our health, our minds, our children—for less crucial concerns like social and career climbing.

But we can't hide imbalance from ourselves. We live in passive desperation. We know we're unstable; we've seen the hundreds of studies on stress and depression to prove it.

> ***In about one third of my cases, the patients are suffering from no clinically definable neurosis, but from the senselessness and emptiness of their lives.***
>
> CARL G. JUNG

We talk about stress and emptiness, but this is usually just talk—"It's bad, yeah, but we can't change it." Well, that's not quite true. We *can* change it. It only takes corrections in our thinking, and thus in our actions. That's all that's necessary for balance in life. There is no magic charm, just the decision of what is important and what isn't.

Reading *The Trees* is to read about backbreaking work and manual labor. Yet it is not a novel about tension, scrambling, lack of time, or lack of meaning. Neither is it about being blitzed with options, doused with formless anxieties, or battered by relentless competition.

Is this the best of times or the worst of times? In our world we worship our work, we work at our play, and we play at our worship. We don't dare look backwards because somebody might be gaining on us. When was the last time we really saw the delicate leaves lacing the trees or really heard the orchestra of bird music in the air? When was the last time we were far enough from a busy street that we could see it from the whimsical perspective of a necklace strung with car-beads?

We can summarize what is wrong with us, and wrong with the society we live in, in two words: *too much*. We could list what we have too much of, but the list itself would be too long.

Life has become to the most of us one swift, headlong race—a continuous fight in which there is so much to do that the half of it has to be left undone. . . . It is not so much what we have done amiss, as what we have left undone, that will trouble us, looking back. ELLEN WOOD

We have lost control of our lives and we are surrounded with counterfeit connections between materialism and happiness. Myriad messages tell us what we should want, what we should buy, and what we should do. We are bombarded with 1,200 advertisements each week, linking carefully created desires to false contentment. We even compete in our cravings. Even when we don't know what we want, we're ready to bite somebody to get it. And we're drifting so far from the real taste of existence that we've begun to *prefer* synthetic living. We are impatient and antagonistic to the idea of taking time, so we sprint through our lives on freeways called Convenience. We look to experts and analysts to think for us, let various reviewers tell us what we like, and even ask artists to do our feeling for us—to agonize and rejoice, to describe the passionate response to life for us so that we can enjoy it at a safer distance.

We now know that it was misguided feminist doctrine that told women they could have it all—and all at once—careers and babies, family and future, marriage and more. It's only logical for both women and men to approach life by dividing it into seasons and focusing certain phases on certain opportunities and priorities that won't ever come back. But books and media keep giving us images of supermoms and do-everything macho-men to keep us feeling guilty and inadequate and dissatisfied.

The least of things with a meaning is worth more in life than the greatest of things without it.

CARL G. JUNG

We must sooner or later learn to put balance ahead of buying and excellence before affluence. This might involve some interesting exchanges, like fewer cocktail parties and more floating in the pool, fewer things and more freedom. Somehow we have to *live out* the most important things.

There is a negative feeling against specialization, however, and against a narrower focus that would allow us to know more about less. There is opposition to ideas like living to work rather than working to live. Our knuckles are rapped if we try to avoid the anxiety and competitiveness of our materialistic society or if we oppose the notion of forfeiting our bodies and spirits and families for something called affluence.

Half of Americans don't get enough sleep. The average couple spends just twelve minutes a day talking to each other. The typical American household is crippled by monetary debt. Is there an alternative?

There is, and it is called simplicity. Simplicity is . . . simple. It involves spending less time at the office and more time with our families, less time in shopping malls and more time outdoors. Consumerism has given us the credit card, but we still we can't buy intimacy and satisfaction with it.

I live by squeezing from a stone
The little nourishment I get.

BESS TRUMAN

Balance, for most of us, sounds pretty good. The balanced life may certainly succeed in the world, yet it isn't likely that it will have a monument named after it. The balanced human being is less than likely to become a first violist with the Boston Philharmonic or earn the Nobel Prize for literature. Not that it's impossible, yet it is more likely that people who pursue such things with all their time and energy will win them.

Having it all can only be a worthy goal if we have it all in balance. What does that mean? It means balancing the finite things, like time, strength, and thoughts, among the seemingly infinite essentials, like satisfying work, family responsibilities, and personal pursuits and obligations. It also means balancing our perspectives and approaches to life between the organized and the spontaneous, between fixed schedules and flexibility. And finally, it implies balancing our achievements with our relationships. Things with people. Getting with being. It involves catering to our preferences and asking ourselves what is really important and whether we are therefore living appropriately.

> ***There must be more to life than having everything!***
>
> MAURICE SENDAK

Putting our overstructured lives back in balance means that we do what has to be done with concentrated attention and care. But we also do what we enjoy doing. It probably means cutting back on work hours for most of us. We must resist the temptation to measure our worth in terms of our output instead of by the quality of our experiences.

Balance almost certainly means reducing the hours we spend watching television. It means giving ourselves more leisure and less idleness. (Note: Finding value in the stillness of the moment is not idleness.) The popular assumption is that no skill is involved in enjoying free time, that anybody can do it. Yet the evidence suggests that free time is more difficult to enjoy than work. Unless we learn to use this time effectively, having leisure at our disposal won't improve the quality of our lives.

> ***There are two things to aim at in life: first to get what you want; and, after that, to enjoy it. Only the wisest of mankind achieve the second.***
>
> LOGAN PEARSALL SMITH

Active leisure doesn't come easily, but before science and the arts became professionalized, a great deal of research, poetry, painting, and musical composition was carried out in free time. All folk art—the songs, fabrics, pottery, and carvings that give each culture its particular identity—is the result of common people striving to express their skills in the time left free from work. Only lack of imagination stands in the way of each of us becoming a poet or a musician, an inventor or an explorer, an amateur scholar, scientist, artist, or collector. We can use our leisure to engage in acts of self-renewal.

> ***One by one the sands are flowing,***
> ***One by one the moments fall;***
> ***Some are coming, some are going,***
> ***Do not try to grasp them all.***
>
> ADELAIDE PROCTOR

Investing energy in relationships is also a good way to improve the balance in our lives. For instance, we can enrich the experience of parenting simply by paying attention to our children, by learning what they are proud of or "into" and then sharing those activities with them.

Imbalance is a waste of life. We must reject the romantic idea of a candle burning at both ends. It is good to journey toward an end, but it is the journey that matters, in the end.

> ***If the texture of our daily life gets any thinner, it'll disappear up its own arsehole.***
>
> NORMA MEACOCK

AFFIRMATION

My aim is to strike just the right balance in my life.

TO THINK AND WRITE ABOUT

To keep your life in balance, it is helpful to keep in contact with yourself. Write, draw, sketch, doodle, and play with your inventiveness in your journal. Take up your pen often, for enjoyment and for self-guidance. Use your journal in any way that seems useful and satisfying at that particular point in time.

You may draw pictures, examine the considerations that complicate a major decision you must make, consolidate what insights you are having about life, copy quotes or tape photos in your book, compose make-believe talks with your wiser self, rehearse what you need to do and say during an upcoming meeting, ask yourself questions and scribble down your intuitive answers, or describe how you feel about those thoughts.

Make your journal a book containing you own unique narrative. Consider these outpourings from your private self, and discover unknown facets of your personality, possibly including preoccupations that you were unaware of. Look for patterns of meaning in your life and secrets of self.

Chapter 12

True Prosperity

Where Wealth Accumulates and Men Decay

The vertue of prosperity is temperance.

FRANCIS BACON

Our financial life does not function separately from the rest of our lives. We may have won the Industrial Revolution, but the spoils of that war soon looked pretty spoiled indeed. For a long time, we have been trapped by our own mistaken certainties, by unconscious and invisible boxes that limit our ability to think of prosperity in realistic ways. It's time we finally understand the role that money should have in the good life.

Most of us believe that prosperity is determined by our net worth, that it is a dollars-and-cents equation: Money = Prosperity. In this system of thought, the more money we have, the more prosperous we will be.

Well, it just isn't true.

Riches are overestimated in the Old Testament: the good and successful man received too many animals, wives, apes, she-goats and peacocks.

MARGOT ASQUITH

True prosperity is having *enough* money to:

- Have time to spend with our families and friends.
- Be able to participate in things we believe are worthwhile.
- Feel satisfied with the contributions we are making to the world.
- Do work that reflects our values.
- Feel that all the pieces of our lives—our jobs, our expenditures, our relationships, our values—fit together to make a prosperous whole.
- Feel at peace about money.

In previous chapters, we discussed our built-in set point called "enough," and how accumulating wealth beyond that point actually lessens our satisfaction. (As a side note: Careful scientific studies have shown that people who win large sums of money in lotteries end up slightly less happy, on average, than they were before.) Ignoring this fact, most of us are still striving to make ever more money, mistakenly believing that wealth will give us a feeling of prosperity. To that end, we have made our jobs the most important factors in our lives. Jobs have replaced family, neighborhood, civic affairs, spiritual concerns, and even marriage as our primary allegiance, our primary source of love and self-expression.

> ***What they do for money dominates their waking hours, and life is what can be fit into the scant remaining time.***
>
> JOE DOMINGUEZ AND VICKI ROBIN

A major source of our discontent is due to advertisements in behalf of consumerism and our own longings for the approval of others. The advertisement/consumerism culture in which we live produces a mass-person, incapable of free choice, incapable of spontaneous, self-directed activities, at best patient, docile, and disciplined to monotonous work, but increasingly irresponsible and finally governed by conditioned reflexes. This is the ideal desired by advertising agencies, sales organizations, and quasi-totalitarian governments. Meanwhile, our human spirits are affronted and humiliated.

We put up with this existence because we think we have no choice. Yet most of us instinctively know there is a better way to live, one that makes sense, that would bring fulfillment and have meaning.

But it is difficult, very difficult, to shrug off the idea that we need "more." Difficult in spite of our knowledge that in striving for more, we are depleting the earth's resources, clogging its arteries, polluting the air, water, and soil. We human beings are our own worst enemies. By ignoring certain fundamental realities, we as individuals, and our economy, are moving dangerously close to the limit of Mother Nature's capacity to handle our demands on her. The vigor of nature is awesome, but its fragility is awful.

> ***Such prosperity as we have known up to the present is the consequence of rapidly spending the planet's irreplaceable capital.*** ALDOUS HUXLEY

But isn't it our right to consume? Don't we have an innate need to gather more and more acorns? This is what we've been led to believe. Along with the notion that money equals prosperity, we also believe that money equals fulfillment—in fact, that money can buy everything, that it can chink all the holes in our psyches.

Let's pretend for a moment that we are at the bottom of society, newly married, poor as church mice. We find minimum-wage work and make enough money to provide for our bare necessities. There is indeed an aspect of fulfillment to our money, for we can see directly that because of it we have food, shelter, and clothing. Money is providing us the means to stay alive.

We work ourselves up the financial scale, until we can afford some amenities, say a television set and a coat purchased in a real store, not a charity outlet. Why, the shopping trips to buy those things, and the money we have for them, that is like being able to select and purchase happiness.

But as our climb up the financial scale continues, eventually we slip beyond amenities into the realm of outright luxuries. At this point, our shopping trips begin to cost us more per "thrill," and the excitement we get from our purchases wears off more quickly. But we don't seem to register that fact.

> ***No one has yet had the courage to memorialize his wealth on his tombstone. A dollar mark would not look well there.*** CORRA MAY HARRIS

Each rung up the ladder of earnings brings more responsibilities and commitments, until one day we come home from work (late) to a 2,000 square foot house (dirty), with a hot tub (broken), and a pool (scummy). Our kids are either "out" (who knows where?) or so glued to some blood-drenched video game that they barely mumble hello. There's no spouse to greet us—we're divorced, naturally. And as we pour ourselves a scotch (no rocks, the ice-maker is on the blink), we fleetingly yearn for the life we had as newlyweds who could find happiness in taking a walk in the park.

Our consumer culture leads us to believe that we might enjoy an ever-higher standard of living without giving up anything valuable, but there is a point at which the money/fulfillment formula stops working for us and starts working against us. In going for the gold, we have sacrificed our relationships with others and our own sense of inner harmony. In order to feel our way back to true prosperity, the critical point for each of us to find is that point at which we have *enough.* Enough for survival. Enough for some comforts. Enough for an occasional luxury. That is the point at which we can optimally appreciate and enjoy our lives. More than that warps the fulfillment factor so thoroughly that it will bend back and bite us.

> ***Most rich people are the poorest people I know.***
>
> ELSA MAXWELL

Beyond enough is identifiable: It's where we begin to accumulate clutter, including cluttered motives. It's bank loans, credit card debts, and unpaid bills. According to Joe Dominguez and Vicki Robin, authors of *Your Money or Your Life,* young Americans currently spend an average of $1.20 for every dollar they make.

Our current money psychology has inflicted on us myths like "economic growth is always good" and "more is better." Spending money is automatic to us. And shopping is an addiction. We have lost the ability to differentiate between a passing fancy and real fulfillment—that point of perfect balance called true prosperity. At that point, any less would not be enough; any more would be too much. Knowing where that point is, and earning and spending only to that point, takes a clear set of values and a strong sense of purpose. It also provides for the makings of a very nice life.

We must learn to evaluate our expenditures in the light of our life purposes. Our purposes are the things we feel passionate about. Passion is the key to distinguishing between purpose and mere material acquisition.

Living at the level of enough, amazing changes will occur not only in our relationship with money but with life itself.

> ***Perhaps the effect wears off in time, or perhaps you don't notice it if you are born to it, but it does seem to me that the climate of richness must always be a little dulling to the senses. Perhaps it takes the edge off joy as well as off sorrow.***
>
> DODIE SMITH

True prosperity is not about budgeting, not about self-condemnation, and not about depriving ourselves. It's about that interesting place at the peak of fulfillment called "enough."

We can never have enough if we are measuring by what others have or think. So what if our siblings or our high-school rivals have "gotten ahead"? We have to be true to our own values and purposes. We also have to reassess our financial choices in terms of sustaining the planet we live on—not just to jump on the environmental bandwagon, but because it makes good sense. What is good for an individual household is also good for the planet.

> ***Wealth, any income that is at least one hundred dollars more a year than the income of one's wife's sister's husband.***
>
> H. L. MENCKEN

What is good for the individual household—and for the individual—is to align our earning and spending with our values and our sense of purpose. Some of us will think alignment seems impossible, considering our particular financial situation. But once we start asking ourselves questions about fulfillment and alignment, we often realize how bored and tired we've been for years. Surely there is more to look forward to in life than the making of more money in order to spend more money?

Living at the peak of the fulfillment curve means always having plenty but never being burdened with excess.

> ***The only thing wealth does for some people is to make them worry about losing it.***
>
> COMTE DE RIVAROL

Frugality isn't a popular word these days. But just because conspicuous consumption is a cross-cultural and historic aberration of the human species doesn't mean that *we* have to fall prey to it. To be frugal means to have a high joy-to-stuff ratio. It also means learning to share, to see the world as "ours," not "mine."

So, we don't go shopping. And before tossing something in the trash, we ask whether there might be another way to use part or all of it. We learn basic living skills through adult-education classes, extension agents, summer residential programs, and books. We borrow these books from the library, of course, instead of buying them. Meanwhile, we learn that a big part of self-respect is self-reliance, knowing that we can take care of ourselves.

We also reexamine our attitudes about buying used items. We eliminate all but perhaps one credit card for emergencies. We assess whether or not we really need that extra car. We select our home and job so that they are within walking distance of each other, and we consolidate errands to reduce the amount of pollution our cars cough into the air. We maintain a proper attitude toward our health, including proper rest. Then we have the time and the energy to play vigorously, amid a lot of laughter.

> ***Money is only money, beans tonight and steak tomorrow. So long as you can look yourself in the eye.***
>
> MERIDEL LE SUEUR

It isn't easy to stop at enough. After all, we want so many things. Advertising isn't to blame for all our desires, either. Human beings are the ever-desirous species. But recognizing that we do want and that no matter how much we get we will continue to want can give us great power. We learn to watch our idle thoughts. We realize that though money is useful, we can't let it use us.

The most ancient priests and prophets knew that human desires are insatiable, but it is still hard for us to believe this is true. It seems so obvious that if we buy just one more thing, that thing we've been wanting, that we'll never want another thing again.

Our desires for more are, however, relentless and unquenchable. They will never disappear. Though it may seem unbelievable, peace of mind—and true prosperity—can result from *renouncing* those desires.

In order to make these changes there is another factor we have to confront. We must look at our work habits. Sometimes we have to question the obvious in order to get at the truth. Our idea of money consists of a patchwork of contradictory beliefs, thoughts, and feelings—notions we absorbed from our parents, our culture, the media, and our life experiences. The same is true of the work we do to earn money.

> ***I simply don't see the point of getting up at six all the time you are young and working eighteen hours a day in order to be a millionaire, and then when you are a millionaire still getting up at six and working eighteen hours a day. . . . What does it all mean?***
>
> NANCY MITFORD

For most of human history, people only worked for two or three hours per day. For the last 200 years, we've shifted back and forth between the forty-hour work week and truly inhuman work hours. We're currently on a swing toward the inhuman side. Just as the computer age most definitely did not bring forth a reduction of paper use, so it has not brought forth a lessening of labor hours. Quite the contrary. We've lost control of our own calendars and the most important possession we have in life—our time.

As a consequence of this increasing workload, we've begun to lose our grip on the family, culture, and community that give meaning to life outside the workplace. Making a living feels like making a dying. When we pick up our paychecks, no matter how large the sum inside, we don't feel we're getting a fair exchange for the investment of *life* we've made. And we're right.

But still we remain enamored with the idea of trying to make more money.

> ***Striving for More is not fun.***
>
> TIMOTHY MILLER

When we shift from living according to others' values (living from the outside in) to discovering and living *our* values (living from the inside out) our jobs, too, may come under consideration. We may discover that we want to spend more hours being good parents, good neighbors, caring friends, loving mates, and good citizens of our planet. We may decide to redefine success for ourselves on a slower track. In fact, we may even reject our infatuation with the idea of making more money.

> ***All prosperity begins in the mind and is dependent only upon the full use of our creative imagination.***
>
> RUTH ROSS

As long as we accept the common belief that more is always better, we will never have enough. Never. On the other hand, true prosperity is empowering; it allows us to take back the power that we have given over to money. This realization can have a potent impact on all aspects of our lives. Other courses open to us. Out of the immense vitalities of our present civilization, a dynamic integration and renewal may take place. This won't come by following the path of least resistance: It will involve nothing less than a change in our total pattern of life.

> ***Money is not everything, but it is better than having one's health.***
>
> WOODY ALLEN

AFFIRMATION

I give myself permission to recognize when I've reached the state of "enough."

TO THINK AND WRITE ABOUT

Think about your latest shopping excursion. Describe it. Description is a reproduction of reality, or at least your view of it. This doesn't need to be a running account of everything you saw, touched, heard, tasted, and felt. Don't describe anything that you don't feel compelled to write about. In that way, your narrative of your shopping experience will have less to do with objective observation than with your individual perception. In other words, don't just try for a verbal snapshot, but record your unique experience, your personal relationship with the experience of spending money and how this enhanced or detracted from your sense of true prosperity.

Part Seven

When We Must Start Over

Chapter 13

SURVIVING DISASTER

A Beam in Darkness: Let It Grow

The best way out is always through.

ROBERT FROST

We *can* surmount the crises of our lives, the catastrophic events, the searing ordeals, the most traumatic experiences life can hold. The sun may fall out of the sky, pulling a curtain of darkness after, but we can nevertheless survive. Parents of cancer-ridden children, targets of rape and assault, victims of crippling accidents and deadly diseases rarely make headlines with their victorious survivals, but survive they do.

Being widowed isn't easy. In fact, though it is a common experience, it is perhaps one of the most difficult challenges in life. The aloneness and sheer size of the loss can be overwhelming.

Divorce can also be devastating. Almost no one makes any preparations for it; we hope it will never happen to us—and when it does, our world is torn apart. How much strain can we take before we break?

To be sure, some experiences are more devastating than others, and the impact of a particular crisis can vary dramatically from one person to the next. The degree of violation we experience individually depends on the meaning of the disaster in our life. But none of us will get through life without being wounded by calamity at some point.

A victim of a fire said, "We went from having a house we'd worked on for twenty years to having twelve grocery bags of stuff and nowhere to live."

> ***There is no limit to human suffering. When one thinks, "Now I have touched the bottom of the sea, now I can go no deeper," one goes deeper.***
>
> KATHERINE MANSFIELD

Former Vietnam POWs report that again and again people say they don't know how these men survived. Most of us are frightened to even think of living through such an ordeal. The men themselves know that there was nothing else for them to do *but* live through it. There simply is no escaping when disaster strikes.

The study of psychology is largely responsible for our tendency to live scared, to expect to crumble in the face of a crisis rather than to surmount it. Of course, disaster has the potential to do us harm. Traumas can plague victims for years. But buried in all of us are undreamed-of powers of healing and growth, even in the face of calamities.

> ***Give sorrow words: the grief that does not speak, whispers in the over-wrought heart and bids it break.***
>
> SHAKESPEARE

How do we live through devastating events and losses? Woody worked for years to become an "overnight success" in a fashionable dance review. Everything looked rosy, until a car hit him as he crossed a busy intersection. He woke in a hospital where he was told that he would walk again, but he would never dance.

"I survived those first days by 'floating.' I just let my mind float. But by keeping my conscious mind floating above what I called 'the abyss,' I was able to function, at least at a surface level, while time alone started to work on the deeper healing. Right then, I couldn't just dive into all that pain. There was too much, I would have been overwhelmed. So I kept above it, and smiled around my gritted teeth."

Trust is fundamental when an abyss opens beneath our feet. Trust in time's healing powers, trust that possibilities for a better future will offer themselves. If we can invoke the courage to wait, simply wait, with our hearts and minds open and expectant, healing and improvement usually come.

Like Woody, we can let go of will, at least for a while, and hold on to trust. We can decide to discover each moment as it comes, instead of trying to manage and control it.

> ***You need not leave your room. Remain sitting at your table and listen. You need not even listen, simply wait. You need not even wait, just learn to become quiet, and still, and solitary. The world will freely offer itself to you to be unmasked.***
>
> FRANZ KAFKA

Communication is another lifeline of survival. In every episode of captivity in recent American history, POWs and hostages have been sustained by ingeniously improvised lifelines of communication. Our relationships are the ties that bind us to life.

Death rates rise sharply for those who need human ties and have none. By unburdening ourselves to another person, we protect ourselves against the potential damages of strain. During times of trauma, we need our friends and families. If we are without a support system strong enough to meet our needs when facing disaster, we have alternatives. Mutual support groups can be very helpful. Group members open up their hearts to each other—and feel relief like sweet air. Cancer patients who are members of support groups fare better than those who don't participate. Alcoholics Anonymous is a famous example of the success of support groups. An array of groups is now available.

Communication heals. Words are medicines that make us whole and keep us whole. If we can't find a friend or a group, we can talk to mental-health professionals, members of the clergy, our own physicians, a sympathetic nurse.

> ***Experience is a good teacher, but she sends in terrific bills.***
> MINNA ANTRIM

Too often, when tragedy first strikes, we are reluctant to voice our inner fears and insecurities to others. But communication at times of distress heals simply by allowing us to put our feelings into words. Communication also helps us recognize that others in similar circumstances have managed to survive. Finally, communication reassures us that our reactions to disaster are natural, that our own distress is actually universal.

> ***Life seems to be a never-ending series of survivals.***
> CAROLE BAKER

Each of our lives is governed by the universal order, but we also have a strong craving for orderliness in our personal environment. Throughout our adult lives, our emotional well-being depends on recurrent and dependable themes, the familiar motifs that give our existence a comforting coherence. This soothing sense of orderliness and regularity is demolished by traumatic events. We truly lose our hold on life. At such times, it is critical to reestablish some order and routine, even if it is only a little corner of our daily life. A small consistency such as keeping a regular dinner time can be consoling—even if we don't feel like eating.

People who triumph over adversity prove to themselves that they do indeed have a degree of command over their destiny. They come out of their trials much stronger than they were before, because now they know that life can't defeat them. We have an astounding capacity to manage our own well-being.

When it is dark enough, you can see the stars.

RALPH WALDO EMERSON

Actress Teresa Saldana survived the vicious stabbing assault that ended her acting career. It seemed to her that nobody could understand how horrifying the ordeal was for her. During her months of recovery, she became convinced that people in similar straits needed an organization to provide emotional support.

Many people struck by tragedy find that the road back to normalcy opens if they work to control and change the social forces that brought them low. Then we have the satisfaction of knowing that others become the beneficiaries of our own healing.

The universe operates through the dynamic of exchange.

Giving and receiving are different aspects of the same flow of energy. By giving, even when we feel we have nothing left, we stimulate the flow that will make us receivers once again. In giving what we seek, we keep the abundance of the universe circulating in our lives. Giving engenders receiving, and receiving engenders giving. What goes out must come back.

If we have our own why *of life, we shall get along with almost any* how.

FRIEDRICH WILHELM NIETZSCHE

Another actor, Tony Danza, lost his mother to brain cancer, despite six months of his daily loving care. Recovering from her death, he took a skiing trip, but his mind was still on his mother. He ran into a tree, collapsing his lung, crushing his ribs, and pulling his leg from his hip socket. A month later, an earthquake destroyed his home. But Tony feels that life is all about looking for "another shot." He found meaning in his personal pain by sharing it with others. He made a film about a son looking after his dying mother, a film that explores the feelings of each. He found a way to make his losses meaningful.

There is no grief that time does not lessen and soften.

CICERO

When trauma first tears into us, surprisingly little attention is paid to our need to find threads of meaning in the tattered fabric of existence. When we suffer pain, the danger of losing our sense of purpose can be profound. Our hunger for meaning is never more urgent. When we can identify a rationale for our anguish, our capacity to endure is significantly increased. People facing even the most horrible experiences are fortified by the conviction that their suffering is not without meaning. How can we find the meaning that we need so desperately? For a surprising number, simply proving that survival is possible is purpose enough. While many give up and plummet into a depression, others find a healing response in fighting their pain and suffering. Others respond by *making* it meaningful.

The world is round and the place which may seem like the end may also be the beginning.

IVY BAKER PRIEST

Some have sustained themselves by working toward a better future while still at the height of their ordeal. Auschwitz survivor Victor Frankl made his trials endurable by looking toward a time when they would assume significance. Sufferers can find salvation through experiencing their ordeal as opportunity: They hope to come out of their experience as different people. For instance, crises can induce a more tolerant and deeper relationship with others. Whatever opportunities seem possible to us, whatever flickering moments of sunlight appear, we should be ready to step into them.

The diamond cannot be polished without friction, nor the man perfected without trials.

CHINESE PROVERB

Many cancer patients, learning of their illness, describe a sudden capacity for gratitude. They feel appreciation for things once taken for granted—eating lunch with a friend, reading a book in a quiet cone of lamplight, raiding the refrigerator for a slice of cake, witnessing the summery beauty of growing grain.

Few people are able to sustain themselves in a crisis with only the belief that "it is God's will." It isn't helpful to be told that there is a higher purpose in our suffering that we can't perceive. If we can't find some unconcealed meaning in the traumatic events, then we must find it in the day-to-day activities of our lives. We don't necessarily have to discover that elusive, ultimate, cosmic meaning of life, but it is therapeutic for us to feel "engaged"—to find something that captures our attention, something that we can pursue passionately.

> ***The deeper the griefs, the greater the joys, when restored to health and favor.***
>
> SAMUEL RICHARDSON

Most of us assume personal responsibility for our fate, even when a loss is clearly due to forces outside ourselves. The impulse to feel accountable surfaces in early childhood and persists throughout our lives. Guilt reactions are displayed by innocent youngsters caught in the crossfire of their parents' divorces, by brilliant students turned down by overcrowded colleges, by people who become seriously ill, suffer accidents, or fall victims to crime. Assuming personal responsibility when misfortune strikes can serve a useful purpose, motivating us to set our lives aright. But there is no cause to throw a blanket indictment over ourselves.

On the face of it, reacting with guilt for our own suffering seems perverse. It is the result of being taught that we will be punished for disobedience or failure. A widow may believe that she is being punished for being a bad wife. Even crime victims fall into this emotional trap, associating their misfortune to some earlier and totally unrelated "bad" behavior. A startling number of physically abused women feel a sense of personal blame.

There is a second reason for assuming blame in the face of misfortune: It helps to satisfy our need to believe that we are in control of our own destiny. The reasoning goes, if we got ourselves into this mess, we can get ourselves out.

> ***The best thing you could do was to give when you had no hope of getting anything in return.***
>
> RICHARD A. STRATTON

However we do it, we must find our grit and form a response to adversity. It can make a difference to our very survival. A willingness to fight back is the kind of behavior that keeps us forging ahead.

The very morning after their release, the fifty-two Iran hostages organized to distribute the gifts and flowers sent to them from around the world to their fellow hospital patients. Their act of kindness was as healing to them as to their beneficiaries. Those traumatized men needed to shift their focus away from themselves. It can be vitally important to stop thinking about ourselves and start thinking of others when disaster strikes. Simple acts of charity help to raise our own power of endurance. After all, we are all brothers and sisters, and we are all suffering in some way.

> ***The testimony of survivors is full of examples of help—men and women giving a vital part of themselves, literally their last reserves, to keep each other going.***
>
> TERRENCE DES PRES

Yet when we first confront our own troubles, thinking of others does not always come easily. Self-interest can't be totally suppressed when crises occur. Yet helping others really is a good thing to do for ourselves. Too much turning inward can put us at risk for becoming professional victims, severing the connection with others that we need.

If we want to begin life again—as victors rather than as victims—the transformation will take place with much more speed when we are consumed by a special mission that takes our thoughts out of our selves. And to one degree or another, a compassionate investment in others is possible for all of us.

But no matter what means we use, it is always best to look suffering straight in the eye, to acknowledge and respect its presence, and then get busy as soon as possible focusing on things we choose to focus on.

Some people look on any setback as the end. They're always looking for the benediction rather than the invocation. But you can't quit.

HUBERT H. HUMPHREY

AFFIRMATION

Though I am grieving, though I am terrified, though I am beset by disaster, I am still alive, and I will endure.

TO THINK AND WRITE ABOUT

Any adversity is worsened if you feel powerless to do something about it. Writing your problems out allows you to take action by focusing your concerns and evoking possible solutions. Explore ways to express every shade of your feelings.

The very act of sitting with your journal signifies your readiness to commune with yourself. The act of writing places you within the mysterious circle of self-healing, no matter what you pen.

Chapter 14

Reinventing Our Lives

I've Died and Come to Life Again

When we walk to the edge of all the light we have and we take a step into the darkness of the unknown, we must believe one of two things will happen—there will be something solid to stand on, or we will be taught to fly. MARTIN EDGES

Common opinion nowadays is that there is no such thing as luck. In the United States especially, we have always liked to believe that our personal actions are all-powerful and that anything is within the realm of possibility. We have a tendency to say we're completely responsible for everything that happens to us.

But sometimes life just happens, for better or for worse: We pursue what we want and often we get it, or at least come close—a top-notch job, a great marriage, an audition with a prestigious ballet company—then suddenly, because of something completely out of our control, we lose everything. Our company downsizes and we're laid off, or we're widowed, or we're the victims of a crime that leaves us crippled. We've played by the rules, done everything right, yet all our hard work means nothing when some force outside us reaches into our lives and snatches our dream right out of our hands.

> ***I am a frayed and nibbled survivor in a fallen world and I am getting along. I am aging and eaten and have done my share of eating too.***
>
> ANNIE DILLARD

Major losses can take the heart right out of us, leaving us with a hollowed sense of identity. We don't know who we are anymore because we can't live as we have in the past. As the first shock of the trauma wears off, people tend to leave us to our own devices. It seems to be over, but we know it's far from over. We're in chaos, moving in mist and tumult. It feels terrible. It's a sick feeling of not knowing, mixed with a feeling of danger. We all have it in ourselves to disintegrate, to reach for the Jack Daniel's, to fall back on self-hatred, madness, carelessness, daylong nightmares, masochism, despair. Can we save ourselves when we are as weak as a blade of grass?

> ***At birth, each of us gets a note slipped under our pillow: "Well, child, have you the courage? . . . The courage to be human? Will the ten thousand things of the world wear you out, blind you, or break your heart? . . ." So the test begins; and it is never completed.***
>
> ERIC MAISEL

A major loss can be the end of an era. There's no bouncing back. We're doomed if we treat what has happened to us like a mere setback. Disaster needs a different kind of attention. It potentially can ruin the rest of our lives. We've given our best and devoted ourselves to our dream. And when we lose it, we're left without a fallback position. For us to start again, we need to be different people.

Some may suggest that we simply try a total change in careers, goals, or lifestyles. That can feel like an insult. It's the same as saying, "Sorry you lost your child, but you'll have another." Some things aren't replaceable. We're not going to get back what we've lost, but we can get our*selves* back.

There are only two directions we can take from right here: backward or forward. Which do we choose? We can't talk ourselves out of a major loss. Our hearts are too independent and too smart to listen. We don't want to take a backward step, but oddly, in order to go forward, first we must go backward. We must grieve, or we can never get beyond the past.

> ***You can't put tears behind you until you've wept them. You can't let go of the past until you've grieved for it.***
>
> BARBARA SHER

What good does grieving do? It won't bring back the past. Nothing will do that. But grieving will give us back our future. Unexpressed pain keeps us captives. By allowing ourselves to grieve we clear the path for better days ahead. Our sense of loss won't go away, but neither will it keep us mined in sorrow.

Just as a broken bone will take its own time to heal, so will a broken spirit. There is no point in our growing impatient, no use in trying to hurry the process. We must shed just as many tears as are needed and not one less. And this is definitely not the time to plan ahead.

Good timber does not grow with ease;
the stronger the wind, the stronger the trees.

J. WILLARD MARRIOT

There is another factor: bitterness. We may have plenty of good reasons to be bitter. The problem arises when we vent it indiscriminately. We may even feel bitter toward the friends trying to cheer us. "The jerks. They just don't understand."

Usually, however, bitterness isn't as authentic as it looks. Believe it or not, one of the reasons we choose to feel bitter is that it's easier than feeling pain. It makes us seem tough. Being bitter gives the illusion that we're fighting, that we're not taking defeat lying down. But bitterness is a log jam. It won't let us get moving.

My mind became feebler as my feelings grew more intense. HECTOR BERLIOZ

But bitterness is something we have to get out of our system. Then maybe we will be ready to move to the next phase: remembering what was wonderful about what we lost.

We need to praise our past. What did we love about it? What were our favorite moments? We must run our minds over our past lovingly. What did it look like, smell like, taste like? How did it feel in our bones? What do we remember loving most of the day-to-day experiences? We must remember our delight in the smallest things.

Letting ourselves describe every lovely detail will give us back something that we have lost. Though at first we may float above it, because it's too painful to remember, eventually we must reclaim it. When we remember that time by praising it, we'll have rescued it, and will be able to take it into the future with us. We must take it with us because we'll never consent to go forward without it.

> ***Three words were in the captain's heart. He shaped them soundlessly with his trembling lips, as he had not breath to spare for a whisper: "I am lost." And having given up life, the Captain suddenly began to live.*** CARSON McCULLERS

It would be impossible to simply forget what we have loved and lost, to just put it out of our memories. It is not helpful for people to tell us to get on with our lives. How ridiculous! We have lost something vital and cherished, and we will always miss it. And that's exactly as it should be. Even if we feel the past somehow betrayed us.

Yes, we may feel that although we loved what we've lost, what we loved failed us somehow. But there is no point in pretending to be indifferent or scornful. In fact, that only hurts ourselves.

It won't break our hearts to remember something that has been snatched away from us. It may *feel* that way. But sometimes feeling that our hearts are breaking is good for us. And eventually we will feel relieved at giving in and remembering.

Our loss might include daydreams we had, even improbable desires, such as being promoted right to the top, marrying an idol, or making a fortune.

After we praise our pasts, we will feel better.

> ***Life, which he had thought worn out and done with, save as a mere mechanical process, seems to have begun afresh for him—life and youth and happiness all renewed together like a second birth.***
>
> MARY ELIZABETH BRADDON

If it's been a while since our loss, realizing that we still grieve can be a revelation. And realizing that there is honor and necessity in grieving allows us to respect our sorrow instead of disparaging it.

There's no doubt it can bring up emotional pain to look back and see what we will never have again. It's hard to look at pictures of people we loved who are now gone. It's the same with dreams we had. It hurts. We fight sorrow as if it will harm us. The opposite is true. Sorrow can heal us. Letting our heart break can be good for us. Most of us fear that if we unleash a great sorrow it will flood and drown us. Any feeling, delayed too long, feels huge and endless. But a decent period of grief can heal a great sorrow.

We might even consider devoting a day of celebration every year to our loss, giving it its due honor.

> ***I have done much rebuilding. To reconstruct is to collaborate with time gone by, penetrating or modifying its spirit, and carrying it toward a longer future. Thus beneath the stone we find the secret of the springs.***
>
> MARGUERITE YOURCENAR

Our next step is to end our resentment toward our present lives. If we've lost big, we may not like our present lives much. We may spend too much time and energy cursing the way things are.

Because the present is all we can imagine, it may seem much uglier than it is. And thinking it is permanent makes it feel intolerable. When we can get somewhat beyond our sense of bereavement, the present won't seem so set in stone. Then we will be able to recognize that this too will pass.

Being at war with our present uses up too much concentration and energy. It's exhausting and distracting. It will do us more good to realize that this phase of our lives is actually a friend. It is like a raft after the sinking of an ocean liner; it may lack the qualities of the cruise we expected, but it's keeping us out of the water.

Suppressing our anger and unhappiness is not an answer. Voicing them provides a much needed release. Of course, we must limit our venting. Eventually, we can turn the complaints around and try to find what's beneficial or good about our present lives.

The no that was hinging over the buildings
Faded like the moon at dawn. YOKO ONO

Without our resentment, we may feel a peculiar emptiness. After all, we at least had the excitement of our anger. It might not have been much fun, but it was a distraction. Without it our days may seem to have no substance; they seem flat and that's frightening in itself.

If you gaze long into an abyss, the abyss will gaze back into you.

FRIEDRICH WILHELM NIETZSCHE

Following a bereavement, moving forward may be as hard as translating a novel in a foreign language. Nothing can be taken for granted. We have to take one step at a time, correcting our ideas again and again, until we've got it the way we want it.

The future may still seem a blank. We don't know anything about it. We don't know what's coming. But we don't have to know. When fate takes the reins out of our hands, we're put in a position we've never been in before. We might even encounter something altogether novel and rare—a totally open mind.

The effects of our losses will surprise us at times. There may be much suffering yet. Still, changes are taking place. We begin to wonder how it will all come out. We can feel as if we have something new and important to learn.

By suffering comes wisdom. AESCHYLUS

Now something unexpected and valuable takes place. Being confronted with our limitations opens us up to a new level of learning.

If there is no wind, row. LATIN PROVERB

When our grieving is done, we naturally begin to look forward again. We discover that we still have our capacity for enthusiasm, for love, for hard work. These haven't been lost. The period of our despair, we discover, was at the same time a period of creative hibernation and development—a kind of purification phase.

New links must be forged as the old ones rust.
JANE HOWARD

We can use touchstones from our past to create our futures. By sifting the essential elements from the ashes of our old lives, we begin to fashion something new. For instance, the actress Teresa Saldana wanted to be a star before she was cut down by a madman with a knife. She liked being in a leading position. She needed a sense of purpose. And she wanted to talk with others. Taking these essentials from her past, she began her new career of helping other victims of crimes. She founded Victims for Victims.

Naturally, this technique is not as easy as it looks. And we may not want to use touchstones from our past; we may prefer to seek all new lives. When Steve lost his home of twenty years, he chose to rebuild a totally different home—"something totally not me." He used his tragedy to rethink the very idea of "home." The fire freed him to take some risks he would never have taken otherwise.

It takes time and course corrections, but eventually our compass needles will fasten on a fixed bearing once again. In our pasts were many forks in the road that we ignored in order to focus on the thing we have now lost. Now we may decide to backtrack and try some of those alternate routes, meanwhile discovering that we are many-faceted.

You often find your destiny on the path you take to avoid it.
CHINESE PROVERB

Often, when a traumatic or catastrophic event occurs, we don't understand its significance. But with time, we will see how the event caused us to grow, even though it was painful. Remember Woody, who dedicated his youth to becoming a dancer? Then a motorist struck him. In one moment, his dream was dashed. Yet he says today that it was the best thing that ever happened to him, because he's now so happy as a choreographer. He's learned that when something seems like the worst thing, it may be the best thing. Everything, even tragedy, can be a gift in disguise. By simply deciding to see possibility, we come through loss with more strength and contentment than we had before.

We can also relax and smell the roses right where we are. We can decide to discover what wisdom there is in living at the shore where fate has cast us. The past is recollection; the future is anticipation; the present is awareness. There is no better time to practice present-moment awareness than when struggling with loss.

Just halfway through life's journey
I reawoke to find myself in a dark wood
Far off course, the right way lost.
How hard it is to tell what this
Wild, harsh, forbidding wood was like
Whose merest memory brings back my fear;
For only death exceeds its bitterness.
But I found goodness there; I'll deal
with that . . .

DANTE

Loss is a great teacher. It offers us a series of weanings, starting in infancy. Each loss pushes us toward realizing that the universe does not revolve around us. Life stretches out for miles in all directions. A fascinating world may be waiting for us to open our eyes and see it.

Once we've lost, we tend to feel that life is over. But it is shocking to realize how much there is left to learn—about ourselves, our lives, and the world. As teenagers, we know everything; by thirty, we know less; by forty, we are brilliantly ignorant. If we are lucky, as we continue to mature, we will grow as ignorant as geniuses and be continuously shaken by what we manage to discover. And each new discovery can be like the earth shifting beneath our feet, like our own amazed, ringing laughter. Like Alice, we can explore every rabbit hole.

We can join Huck and ride the river. We can discover the essence of poetry, unravel the mystery of song, grasp the intricacies of color. We can live as explorers.

> ***Surviving meant being born over and over.***
>
> ERICA JONG

We are strengthened when we learn to acknowledge the world the way it is and to accept our loss as one of the conditions we have to live with.

> *Pity the man who has lost his path and does not follow it and who has lost his heart and does not know how to recover it. When people's dogs and chicks are lost they go out and look for them and yet the people who have lost their hearts do not go out and look for them. The principle of self-cultivation consists in nothing but trying to look for the lost heart.*
>
> MENCIUS

AFFIRMATION

I acknowledge my loss and affirm that I can continue to function and even to overcome this sense of blankness.

TO THINK AND WRITE ABOUT

One way out of an overwhelming sense of chaos is to become conscious of how your mind is really working, how one thought is actually leading to another at the subconscious level. What you ordinarily don't admit to consciousness is enlightening when brought to the surface. Experimenting in your journal with forms of free-intuitive writing can take you to very different levels. It may throw light on the relationships between your thoughts, feelings, actions, and sensations, and how these interact with the outside world in the context within which you now find yourself. Your writing may even overlap into catharsis.

If you feel more inclined to draw a picture, do so. One journalist in the process of reinventing herself drew a deserted farm, with a forsaken shed leaning tiredly toward a weed-filled garden. That was how she felt about herself and her life. Recognizing the feelings of fatigue, abandonment, and encroaching waste, she was able to move toward energizing herself, getting the care she needed, and reseeding her "garden."

You don't have to be a physiologist to keep physically fit, nor do you have to be a psychologist to keep psychically fit. If you allow yourself to truly let go of directing your thoughts, you may experience a flash of understanding. Beyond bringing a calming effect, such journal work can provide a basis for self-knowledge at a deep level.

Part Eight

Bearing Up Against Time

Chapter 15

Facing Middle Age

A Second Blooming

Perhaps middle-age is, or should be, a period of shedding shells; the shell of ambition, the shell of material accumulations and possessions, the shell of the ego. ANNE MORROW LINDBERGH

Though the common idea is that by middle age all the juice is gone from life, when we reach this stage we may be delighted to find ourselves juicier than ever. Middle age is a time of ripeness. As we reach our fiftieth year, we discover that midlife is unlike anything we imagined.

Middle age is a time of great learning and great opportunity. We are at ease now with finding our way as we go, with creating new ways for ourselves.

The average woman in the U.S. and Canada can expect to live almost thirty years past menopause—a

span of years that she wants to make as healthy and productive as possible.

THE UNVIERSITY OF CALIFORNIA AT BERKELEY WELLNESS LETTER, OCTOBER 1995

We may have feared middle age. Middle age looked settled, it looked answered, it looked finished, it looked . . . old. It was not a time when people were still changing, still becoming. Middle age was where our parents lived—but we're not that old yet! How can we not be old and be middle-aged at the same time? And what does being middle-aged mean if it doesn't mean being old?

It means we've reached the harvest years. We've worked hard at discovering and accepting who we are, at reconciling the paradoxes in our lives, at learning to recognize true success and to live with disappointment and loss. We've become masters at finding ways to detach without losing our sense of where we are and what's gone by and what's still to come, of learning to take responsibility for ourselves and do what we can for others.

Middle age means time is now a real factor, however. We don't have an endless amount of it left. We can foresee the end, almost hear it, like a distant mutter of thunder. That knowledge awakens a certain caution. Those who sail out far from the nearest harbor may never find solid ground again. Those who bet everything on a single course may lose everything. But maybe we don't have to take all-or-nothing risks anymore. We realize that achieving "it" is not so important anyway, playing the game is.

This is what fifty* looks *like!

GLORIA STEINEM

We're middle-aged all right, but middle-aged isn't what we expected, especially if we expected a predictable future, the end of experimentation, and the start of a fixed point of view. We're likely to be less stressed, though our days are fuller. We are lonely at times, though we prefer to be alone. We dislike change yet we want to try new things. We feel more content, though we're more anxious about what's ahead.

We know what is possible and what is not, we accept limitations while being willing to challenge them, and we know we might not succeed or that success might be different from what we thought. And we understand that we are responsible for ourselves.

Still, when we blow out the candles on our fiftieth-birthday cake, we find we're not ready to be this old. We don't look old, and we certainly don't act old. Yet suddenly we're getting offers for senior discounts—and lots of life-insurance mail. Addressed to us?

> ***With the beginnings of the middle years, we face an identity crisis for which nothing in our past has prepared us.***
>
> JANET HARRIS

Middle age feels like another one of those awkward stages. Reluctant as we may be, we have another phase of in-between years to go through. We're presented with another opportunity to transform ourselves, much as during our adolescence. Once again we must put up with physical changes and emotional upheavals. That's the downside. The upside is that we get another chance to define who we are. Not old, not young, the blurring of the lines creates just enough confusion to allow a metamorphosis.

It's shocking to experience the perception the world has of us now—as older. The first glimmer may come when we go to a new doctor who seems too young to be practicing medicine. Who is this child with a dimpling smile and blinking eyes? Can she really know anything?

Or it may come with a difference in the way others behave toward us. They may treat us with *respect*. Or as if we're invisible, their eyes floating over us. "Ah, it's only a middle-aged person, of no consequence."

> ***It is middle age that has widened and lengthened, so that most people's fifties and sixties can be described as an unremarkable—and therefore quite remarkable—continuum of high-energy living.***
>
> LETTY COTTIN POGREBIN

If we tell our age, we don't want to be believed. We want people to think of us as younger. That's the way we think of ourselves. We also misgauge other people's ages. In meeting a woman, we suppose she's close to our age, and then learn she's ten years younger. It's worse when we meet someone we assume is older than us only to discover he's actually our same age. We make these errors because of our mental image of a middle-aged person. When we were children, we thought of fifty as old, with gray hair and wrinkles. Probably crocheting doilies or whittling whistles for grandchildren. "Middle-aged" meant orthopedic shoes, support stockings, square bodies, and cholesterol tests.

> ***One searches the magazines in vain for women past their first youth. The middleaged face apparently sells neither perfume nor floor wax. The role of the mature woman in the media is almost entirely negative.***
>
> JANET HARRIS

We thought that by the time we reached our fifties we would have changed in the way we looked, the way we dressed, the way we behaved. When did we get the idea that people our age were always quiet and circumspect, couldn't wear short shorts and halter-tops anymore, didn't enjoy sexy movies, and only read Reader's Digest condensed books—in the large-print editions? From where did those wild notions arise?

And how did so many things we have lived through get to be history: Jim Jones and the Jonestown suicides, the first black woman to become Miss Universe, the New York City blackout, Legionnaires disease, the life and death of Howard Hughes, Watergate, Wounded Knee, and the exile of Aleksandr Solzhenitsyn? We can remember when O. J. Simpson was just a halfback, when Lt. William Calley was found guilty of the My Lai massacre, when Lew Alcindor changed his name, when Popeye was popular, when TV sets were rare.

I am continually amazed at how old young has become . . . Now all of a sudden, I'm older than my parents were when I thought they were old.

LOIS WYSE

As we've reached middle age, we've also invented the New Age. We're troubled for the first time by an awareness of our mortality. We begin to realize how many people have lived and died before us over the centuries, people who lived as passionately but faded into the blue evening light. It's sobering to realize that one day we, too, will be among those cadres of the long dead and forgotten.

Why, we're fifty! We're beginning to have *infirmities.* And for women, there is "the change of life."

Part of us feels very young, but those reminders that we're not keep popping up. We're bothered by the slackening of our bodies. We work out, but still we're not quite lean or mean. Our faces are beginning to deteriorate. Our hair is thinning or turning gray. Our eyelids sag. Our frown lines are deeper. Our upper arms are too fleshy for sleeveless shirts.

> ***Middle-aged rabbits don't have a paunch, do have their own teeth and haven't lost their romantic appeal.***
> AURELIA POTOR

The physical changes are only, as they say, skin-deep. Other changes are less obvious but more worrisome. For instance, we can exhaust ourselves doing an ordinary day's work. We can no longer party all night, play tennis in the morning, and have energy left over. And we get tired differently now. It affects us mentally as well as physically. Too much mental effort, and we can feel brain-dead.

In earlier eras, women's lives ended soon after the reproductive years came to a close. Without today's nutritional advantages, up-to-the-minute medical care, and the wonders of the machine age, there was little chance to refeather an empty nest. Even so, it's hard to be grateful for menopause.

For one thing, women beyond a certain age are considered beyond sensuality as well. This is most evident in the media. Older men, like Warren Beatty and Harrison Ford, regularly play opposite much younger actresses, like Halle Berry and Anne Heche. It's accepted without question. But poor Mrs. Robinson is still a bad joke. Maturity and experience aren't considered assets if we're female and fifty. One of our goals may be to change this popular concept, so that our real vibrancy and capacity for passion can be recognized. At the very least, we can't allow ourselves to believe were anything less than sexy.

Today's grandmothers don't look like grandmothers. They look like women. LOIS WYSE

Today's grandmothers wear leather jackets, platform boots, and hemp bracelets. They look fabulous. So do today's grandfathers in blue jeans, sweatpants, and jogging shorts. We're surfing the Web, and we've asked for a pair of inline skates for our birthday.

When a woman ceases to alter the fashion of her hair, you guess that she has passed the crisis of her experience. MARY HUNTER AUSTIN

We are middle-aged, and yet there is still some life left in us. If we're not quite up to dancing the night away, we still manage to enjoy ourselves, to find a few laughs. After all, we still have a lot to discover and experience and reflect upon. We muse about the adventures still to come. The wrong thing at this point would be to stop learning, stop growing, stop testing our limits. We no longer have to answer to anyone, to explain ourselves, to impress other people. After fifty years of life, we are finally free to be ourselves. We also know more, and are better able to make sense of what we know. At times, we even gain that rare field of vision that shows us our importance in the scheme of things and give us an understanding of ourselves and our relationships, and what we can really hope to do in our lives. Those moments are gratifying. And relieving. And to think it only took us half a lifetime to achieve them.

Since more than half my hopes came true
And more than half my fears
Are but the pleasant laughing-stock
Of these my middle years . . .
Shall I not bless the middle years?
Not I for youth repine
While warmly round me cluster lives
More dear to me than mine

ANNE BRONAUGH

But getting older is only one part of aging. The other parts are about learning and experimenting and continuing to grow. Getting older is getting another helping of life. Another chance to do and be whatever we want to do and be. We can't quit living before our time is up. This season of our lives presents yet another passage, which if we accept its challenges, can give us new insights.

A great deal of our time has been spent in calculating just what we wanted when we grew up. No we're grown. And this is the new age of old age. In this country and this era, we have the possibility of better health for more years than any other generation in history. Why, even our parents have transformed themselves into "senior citizens" living in "active retirement" instead of being old people waiting for the end.

At fifty, we have a good twenty years of productive work before our own senior years. Why, that's time enough to do almost anything.

It's so horrible to be, oh God, thirty*. . . . Today is the beginning of the end. It's pushing forty—and menopause out there waiting to spring—and*

before you can even turn around you're a senior citizen. MURIEL RESNIK

We're fifty, but we still want to leave our mark, our footprint on the earth, something that says "I was here." We want to participate actively in important affairs. We want to feel passionately. We have more things we want to do than we have time in the day to do them.

From one point of view, it's sad that we finally get so many wonderful insights about how to live only when we get halfway through our lives. But wait a minute. Here is a novel idea: What if the only point of life is to learn how to live it well? Meanwhile, knowing at last that *life is its own purpose,* we look forward to experiencing every moment as fully as possible.

AFFIRMATION

As I progress through my middle years, I look forward to finding my way as I go, perhaps even creating new ways for myself.

TO THINK AND WRITE ABOUT

You may feel ambivalent about reaching middle age. There are pros and cons to being this old. Imagine a conversation in which you allow different viewpoints to speak to one another frankly—and to listen to one another attentively. It can be remarkably revealing.

Write a dialogue between your young self and your middle-aged self. Every normal person has conflicting attitudes and points of view within his personality. Being of one mind is more easily achieved if you can openly observe your conflicting thoughts and encourage them to mesh. You split yourself in your journal conversation in order to hash out a cooperative agreement. Such an exercise helps you move closer to a healthy solidity of mind.

Chapter 16

Caregiving

Our Love Outlasts the Years

Ever' man wants life to be a fine ting, and a easy. 'Tis fine, boy, powerful fine, but 'tain't easy. Life knocks a man down and he gits up and it knocks him down agin. I've been uneasy all my life.

MARJORIE KINNAN RAWLINGS

While some things take years to learn, middle age too often offers us a short course in elements with which we may feel uneasy—elements like life and death and the gray place between them.

Mike learned about these things when his mother suffered a massive stroke. She was almost completely paralyzed and was placed in a skilled nursing facility. Though conscious, she couldn't even lift a cup of water to her mouth. Someone had to tip the liquid down her throat for her. Mike and his father visited her every day. This was time-consuming enough, but Mike soon found he had to do more for his father, too. The elderly man's emotional and physical strength was being tested to the ultimate, and he needed Mike's help with everything from mowing his lawn to preparing his meals.

It is a sad fact that when we reach middle age, just when we've got our own nests emptied, we often must begin to parent our parents. Then we have to learn the hard way about hospitals and life-and-death decisions. When the parents who have always been our guides become elderly and perhaps ill, we can expect to go through several stages of adjustment. The process is similar to grief, though we don't get the support from others that grief due to death garners.

For each of us, after middle-age, the world is always emptying. DAISY, PRINCESS OF PLESS

Our first reaction to a parent's infirmities is probably shock. We are likely to rationalize away symptoms of our parents' illnesses for as long as possible. This defensive posture is usually transitory, and it serves a purpose: It cushions the blow. When we're no longer able to deny the facts, we may feel angry and resentful. If we know where to get them, the help and sympathy of friends and professionals can be a great comfort.

As we begin to accept the truth that our parents' health is failing, powerful emotions may be released within us—more anger, but also guilt. The medical world in which we begin to move is foreign terrain to us, and its citizens use a vocabulary we may not recognize. And decisions abound. It is in making these decisions for our parents that more guilt is triggered, because we never stop being our parents' children.

It is up to us to get the help we need to get through the process of reconciling ourselves to a parent's last years. We must acquaint ourselves with the medical community by visiting available social workers, psychologists, and clergy. Helpful resources may include community-crisis centers or private therapists. We may also need help from a financial adviser.

> ***No man, not even a doctor, ever gives any other definition of what a nurse should be than this—"devoted and obedient." This definition would do just as well for a porter. It might even do for a horse.***
>
> FLORENCE NIGHTINGALE

We won't be able to do it by ourselves. It is essential to try to find a balance, to be fair to ourselves even as we care for our failing parent. Friends, family, neighbors, volunteers, and professionals can all be a help. In Mike's case, a neighbor of his parents was a welcome source of support for Mike and companionship for his father.

One of the prime causes of exhaustion when a parent needs us at this time sounds trivial when verbalized: We get worn out simply running errands. There are sources of help available even for this mundane but draining chore, however. We can look into community-subsidized transportation for the elderly and disabled. Counseling and other assistance may be available through nearby colleges with home-health programs. Public health agencies may offer cleaning and shopping services. Programs such as Meals-on-Wheels can provide food and some drugstores deliver.

Sharing our pain and our insights with others can help everyone learn better methods of providing for failing loved ones. Such groups can also provide crash courses in long-term care.

It's important that we set our areas of responsibility. This helps with our struggle to meet the needs of our loved ones, our families, and ourselves.

Compassion is an alternate perception.

M. C. RICHARDS

It's also important to learn to relax.

The last thing Mike wanted to hear when he felt wound up tight was his wife's urge to "calm down." But relaxation is one of the most obvious ways in which we can make ourselves feel better in stressful situations. It is a skill that can be learned.

"Why bother?" Mike said. Well, because tension is painful and unpleasant. Mike lay awake at night feeling tired, tense, and worried about his parents. He made every possible effort to switch off and relax only to find that the harder he tried the more elusive such a peaceful state seemed to be.

If we have no experience in it, learning to relax takes time at first, about half an hour a day for a few weeks. (Often women have the advantage over men in this case, for they learn relaxation techniques in natural-childbirth classes.) The general method is to lie down comfortably, feet about twenty-four inches apart, hands palm up about twelve inches from our sides. When settled, start to work through the body's muscles one by one, tensing them hard and then releasing that tension completely.

You must learn to be still in the midst of activity and to be vibrantly alive in repose.

INDIRA GANDHI

By the end of the first week, we should feel a noticeable progress. After a few weeks, we can shorten the exercise gradually. At the same time, we can practice relaxation in increasingly difficult situations. We should develop the habit of checking our tension level frequently and relaxing when we need to. We can give ourselves a quick relaxation "fix" by tuning into our breathing. Take a deep breath, hold it, then say "let go" as we breathe out.

Relaxation is an attitude, a habit, and a restorative, as well as a skill. During difficult periods of our lives, we need the ability to adopt a relaxed posture, stop rushing about, and make a habit of doing things we find relaxing. We can also seek out pleasures and treats for ourselves, and just plain give ourselves a break. The sense of helplessness recedes as we gain a sense of control over our lives again. The feeling of being out of control in itself creates stress.

Meanwhile, of course, we are doing everything we can to brighten the days of our failing loved ones, making them feel they are still part of the living world. But unrelenting optimism can make them feel isolated. They may long for the chance to air their true feelings. It doesn't do them any good to have us tell them, "Don't talk like that," when they speak of coming to the end.

> ***The longest day must have its close—the gloomiest night will wear on to a morning. An eternal, inexorable lapse of moments is ever hurrying the day of the evil to an eternal night, and the night of the just to an eternal day.***
>
> HARRIET BEECHER STOWE

We must also guard against being overprotective. A velvet-glove treatment that avoids the bad news of daily life will leave our loved ones feeling frustrated. After all, they aren't dead yet! We should allow them to participate in life as much as they are willing for as long as they can, the same as we would want to do ourselves.

This is a time to take especially good care of ourselves, however. We can be of no help if we get ill. We should also try our best to keep up our personal and family routines.

Various daycare centers for adults provide respites for caregivers. Public and private health agencies and in-home nursing services also provide respite care. We shouldn't feel guilty for seeking respite, either. In fact, our failing parents may want a respite from *us* now and again.

> ***We could only be to each other what any two human beings might be, close or far, quick or dull, yielding or hard.***
> HELEN YGLESIAS

If we are suddenly required to make decisions for a parent whose illness has rendered him incompetent, the task may be overwhelming. If we've given him the chance in the past, our parent may have spoken of his wishes about such things as "heroic efforts" to keep him alive. If not, and if the parent is comatose or terminally ill, now is the time when we must look to our own ethics to help us with issues of death and dignity. Patients in a state of permanent unconsciousness are said to be in "a persistent vegetative state." They are unaware of their surroundings and can no longer experience pain or pleasure. Researchers have found that most Americans support such a patient's right to die. Most of us fear and oppose the intrusion of life-support technology into these most private moments. However, life-and-death decisions are always going to be difficult.

> ***Multitudes, multitudes in the valley of decision.***
> JOEL 3:14

The deaths of our parents present us with an inevitable fact of life. If psychological issues have been left unresolved, we may feel guilt and remorse. Those of us who make efforts to resolve issues before the death of someone we love are rewarded. These issues may include confronting unresolved problems, understanding our failing parents' importance in our life, and gaining more sympathy and understanding of our parents as people. We can't change the past, but we can get rid of a lot of frustration. As an example, never saying "I love you" to a parent is high up on the list of regrets people have once that parent dies. Whatever we think we would like to tell our parents on their deathbeds, we should say to them today. We may never get another chance.

> ***Why didn't children ever see that they could damage and harm their parents as much as parents could damage and harm children?***
>
> LAURA Z. HOBSON

What are some other practical things we can do to ease our emotional pain and depression during this difficult time? Well, we can get outdoors into the fresh air at least once a day, regardless of what we do there. Or at least sit in the sunlight of a sunny window as much as possible, especially in winter. We can bring green plants, flowers, or pets into our home. Living things force us to think of life. We can also spend time with children; they shed sunshine on our thoughts. We should exercise every day. Exercise acts as a buffer against stress and can help protect our cardiovascular and immune systems from the effects of stressful events. Taking control of our own health also offers psychological benefits. Wallowing in self-pity isn't helpful, but we can be gentle with ourselves, and give ourselves treats—a movie, a massage, a shopping excursion, a sporting event. This is a time to balance solitude with social occasions.

We must also confront the conspiracy of silence, if we experience that. People may not mention our parent for fear of upsetting us. We have to tell our families and friends that it is important for us to talk about the person we love, because she is very much on our mind.

Reducing the use of alcohol is important now. Excessive consumption of alcohol will only increase a tendency to depression. Instead of relying on drink, we can put ourselves in the presence of beauty and grace.

> ***The circle comes around for everyone. It dips, but it comes round. . . . Never knew anyone didn't have the balloon go up and down.*** RUTH GORDON

Also important is reliving happy memories. We should pick special memories of past times spent with our parent and recall them fondly.

We can't forget the rest of our families. They, too, need to talk, and we must listen to them, especially our children.

Laughter and crying are the most effective natural releases of the painful emotions of fear, anger, and sadness. Ranting and raving help release tensions, too, but we must choose our times and our audiences wisely. We may find relief by screaming in our car while alone. Punching a heavy bag or pillow, or spending an hour in a batting cage is also useful. Similarly, we can rent a movie that makes us cry. Afterward, we will feel tired—but clear again.

People who hold in their frustration and anger usually

develop guilt. And depression can take hold if we fail to acknowledge or discuss our sadness. Depression may deepen our personality, however, leaving us better able to cope with future problems. It is healthiest to express our feelings, whatever they are, and to forgive ourselves for them, because anger and guilt that we do not release can turn into hostility and resentment.

It takes time to accept the fact that our parents cannot be healthy and mentally agile forever. We must remember that pain is always inevitable when we love people.

> *Even, odd—black, white—life, death—father, son. The cycles continue!*
>
> JOYCE CAROL OATES

AFFIRMATION

I will be as kind to myself as I am to my parents in this time of caregiving.

TO THINK AND WRITE ABOUT

Imagining an alternate viewpoint can help you come to a new understanding, even when you are stressed by giving care to others. For example, when you feel you are at loggerheads with the parent you are trying to help, you can use the technique of altered point of view by writing out the situation from your parent's point of view, using "I," as if you were her. In this way, you might very well tap into a brand new understanding of your parent's reasoning and attitudes.

This technique has other benefits. It can even allow you to take yourself out of your difficult situation—for a little vacation, as it were. Whisk yourself away to another place or time altogether. If it is winter where you are, write yourself into a place where the hills are frosted with green. If you are in the midst of sultry summer, write about the beat of rain on a distant roof.

Or, you might pretend you're in the future and can see the results of your actions today. This can help you anticipate how your current decisions will impact your life later. Or help you predict where your current attitudes may lead you.

Part Nine

The Ebb Tide

Chapter 17

LIFE EXPANSION

When You Are Old and Gray and Full of Sleep

I believe we make two basic errors when we consider ambition in older people. One is that we mistake their great calmness about winning and losing—which comes from long experiences with these events through their lives—with lack of interest in what happens.

GILBERT BRIM

In our dreams, we are always young. Nonetheless, the aging process befalls us all. Some can tolerate its predicaments and live with them for decades without suffering great hardship. Remaining flexible is the secret. Learning the art of growing old should be considered one of our greatest accomplishments.

Very old age is actually very new. There has never been anything like it before. There have been old people, but not many. In 1900 there were 123,000 persons in America over eighty-five years of age. Now there are over three million. By the year 2050, some estimates predict as many as fifty million elderly.

In the past, death occurred with random regularity, so that growing old was an accident, a survival based on chance. Today, most people expect to live to about seventy-five years. We have another season of life, another flowering time.

> ***I want to be thoroughly used up when I die, for the harder I work, the more I live. Life is no "brief candle" to me. It is a sort of splendid torch which I have got hold of for a moment, and I want to make it burn as brightly as possible before handing it on to future generations.*** GEORGE BERNARD SHAW

We seem to avoid the subject of old age, though. The youth cult is not a twentieth-century fixation; aging has always been taboo. We tend to deal with it only in the abstract. It is a part of life that rarely attracts artistic or literary attention. As far as films go, aging is not good box office—unless the characters are portrayed in the comic-sentimental mode, making their age easy to swallow.

Yet the fact is we have a new life segment—a third age—bringing new decades of opportunity. This new age as yet lacks definition—biological, economical, or political. We have no encyclopedias, textbooks, experiences, or models to guide us.

How long do we expect to live? Several lines of evidence place the natural human life span at a remarkable 120 years. In 1994, newspapers in Oakland, California, reported that a man lived to 124. In Japan, Shigechiyo Isumi lived to be 121. What is possible for one is possible for others.

Quite a leap from the century of the first Roman Caesar, when human life expectancy was twenty-five years.

Of course, there are huge differences in individual processes of aging. Our age is expressed in years, by the sum of our birthdays, only because no other simple standard is available. But the speed of aging varies tremendously in different individuals.

We cannot paint our Mona Lisa *and leave the last third of the canvas blank. We cannot build our house and leave off the roof. We cannot run our race and stop before the final lap. We cannot have dinner without dessert. We cannot sing our Battle Hymn without the "Glory, Glory, Hallelujah." We should sing all our song.* WALTER M. BARTZ II

Though the fountain of youth is still a dream, there is little doubt that our aging can be delayed for appreciable periods of time these days. Our personal task in growing old is to learn to stay young throughout our old age, or, as one ancient Greek philosopher said, to die as late as possible. A glowing autumn of life is not merely the product of luck or fortuitous medical breakthroughs alone. Merely staying alive isn't enough; we have the opportunity of pioneering a new way to be old.

As in every other stage of life, what happens to us as we age matters far less than how we respond to it.

To know how to grow old is the masterwork of wisdom, and one of the most difficult chapters in the great art of living. HENRI-FRÉDÉRIC

Often, thoughts about aging focus on economic security and independence. But that's not enough. We need something to live on to be sure, but more importantly, we need something to live for. As desirable as the prolongation of life may seem, it doesn't in itself form a blessing. Unless we use the extra years well, they are simply surplus. Life extension should be life *expansion,* a sounder, richer, and fuller experience than when we were busy earning a living and rearing a family.

In our senior years, as in all the stages of life, the art of living is a matter of cultivating our potentials. It is a commitment to human values. In the art of aging, the art of living reaches its highest level. Wise aging is the art of the possible.

In many people, the machine age has produced the belief that even we are mechanical instruments that follow a prearranged pattern. The established pattern is that old people are afflicted with chronic ailments, and this is our time to rest. But we all know the relationship between rest and rust. Ironically, too much rest may exhaust our strength. The fight against becoming seatbound is an important factor in successful aging.

> ***Exercise can preserve something of our early strength even into old age.*** — CICERO

Another rewarding activity deserves recognition for its therapeutic value: Twenty-six muscles are set in motion by the act of laughing. Besides the facial muscles, it thoroughly activates the muscles of the diaphragm, thorax, and intestines. And the air exchange in the lungs is multiplied about seven times.

> ***The best tunes are played on the oldest fiddles.*** — SIGMUND Z. ENGEL

Being old isn't necessarily easy, though we may not have to work anymore. A culture that equates material possessions with success, and views the frantic, compulsive consumer as the perfect citizen, can afford little space for aged human beings. We are past competing; we are out of the game. Unfortunately, our culture endorses human obsolescence. Because of that, when we are old, we are often hesitant about exercising our right, possibly our duty, to contribute the wisdom of our experiences. We tend to draw into ourselves and keep our own counsel. We are inevitably self-conscious of our age as it separates us from the rest of the population.

> ***But when you get to be our age, everyone keeps expecting you to die. That gets mighty annoying!***
>
> SARAH AND ELIZABETH DELANY

When we don't assert ourselves, we live in a limbo of our own making. Our world narrows. Friends die, others move away, some become too frail to receive us, or we become too frail to see them. Under these circumstances, it is sometimes hard to envision a glorious old age. There is, however, one easy bridge we can establish, especially if we are grandparents, and that is relationships with the very young. Both sides of that alliance feel themselves outside the rational, competitive world of the intervening generations.

But we can't stop there. If the world won't accept our value, we have to champion it ourselves. We know we have wisdom; no one lives for the better part of a century without picking up a lesson or two. And we know the world needs all the insight it can get.

What is wisdom? Is it knowledge? Good judgment? Seasoning? If these qualities are combined with humanity, humility, and humor, real wisdom comes into being. When possessed, it is the greatest asset of old age. With wisdom we can continue to be useful members of our society, and we can also master the psychological burdens of our years. We can revel in our sense of worth, and make our leisure productive. We can cultivate new interests and nourish our inquisitiveness.

> *For age is opportunity no less*
> *Than youth itself, though in another dress,*
> *And as the evening twilight fades away*
> *The sky is filled with stars, invisible by day.*
>
> HENRY WADSWORTH LONGFELLOW

What we don't use, we lose. This is true of our brain as well as of our muscles. Only the widest array of interests will preserve our mental functions. Learning new things will even extend them. It is silly to tell ourselves that an old dog can't be taught new tricks; that's not even a half-truth.

We are the healthiest, fittest, longest-lived people in history. In 1900 the average U.S. citizen was dead by age forty-nine; fifty was considered old age. We now expect to live thirty or more years beyond that. How astounding! A vastly expanded horizon stretches before us. We have every reason to feel grateful. Instead of complaining about our age, we ought to be reveling and relishing this extra time.

Yet negative feelings descend on many of us, a sense of insignificance, a belief that we're washed up, out of time, close to death. Again, this is a matter of choosing whether to see the glass as half-empty or half-full. The positive new reality is that we have bonus years to fill to the brim.

I can't give you a recipe to live long, life is how you live, how you sleep, how you eat, how you drink, how you work, life is what you are. DORA ZINS

Time is all any of us have. Chunks of time—minutes, days, months. They are the building blocks of being, the containers we can stuff with pleasure, loving, doing, and caring. Life is not numbers of years but hours of being, not age but time.

All of us, however brightly burning, agree about one fact concerning our elder years: We share a sense of time passing constantly faster. The passing seasons loom larger. If life is time, we must seize it as if we have every right to it. We must take it in, hold it, expand it, shape it to our dreams. People who love life control their time to whatever degree possible. They try to multiply their years on earth by adopting healthier lifestyles, and they try to expand each unit of time by living it intensely and attentively.

The way to slow time down and prevent our years from racing off is to introduce more newness into our living, more firsts of the sort we experienced in childhood when everything was fresh and when time itself looked eternal. More challenges and unfamiliar encounters, the surprises that bring time to a standstill. More savored moments. More noticing. More remembering as well, for the nourishment of nostalgia at this stage in life is underrated.

After age sixty, in ten minutes more you are eighty-five. DON MARQUIS

Paying attention gives us more time, which explains the profound importance of mindfulness as a means of extending life and elongating time. To be mindful is to be conscientiously alert, in control, and open to life's potentiality. Experimental studies have shown mindfulness to improve health, augment brain development, improve eyesight and hearing, reduce depression, boost self-confidence, and lengthen life. Can we afford not to practice it?

Living mindfully asks nothing of us but a commitment to *intentionality*. It requires no effort other than purposeful concentration and the boldness to live each day with aim and awareness. It means being both fully engaged in the present and actively in touch with the past. Accomplishing that, we trick time into slowing and delivering us more life.

Living mindfully also helps us avoid being one of those people who are caught by surprise when it is time to die—since they have allowed themselves to live so little.

One of the most important tenets of the art of living is the ability to create joy in our lives. When we get old, everyone starts to worry about us. "Don't do this, don't do that." As a consequence, we have low expectations of joy. We forget how to laugh in our stomachs (exercising those twenty-six muscles).

Being with friends and in relationships with others is central to putting joy in our lives.

> ***If I don't enjoy myself now, when shall I?***
>
> OMAR KHAYYÁM

Life is a fatal disease. Once contracted, there is no hope for survival. But must it end before it really ends? *Use it or lose it*. Contained in that sparse statement is immense and pervasive wisdom. A still stream stagnates. That is a powerful and universal truth. Without the energy of flow, every form of matter, every order of life, deteriorates. The relationship between disuse and decay is closely linked.

With easy logic, we identify ourselves as *Homo sapiens,* which, roughly translated from the Latin, means "thinking man." The most powerful computer has a storage capacity and information-processing rate between 1,000 to 10,000 times *less* than our brain. We're carrying around an amazing amount of head power. And deprived sensually, nutritionally, socially, or emotionally, we are shockingly at risk.

> *Live all you can; it's a mistake not to. It doesn't so much matter what you do in particular so long as you have your life.* HENRY JAMES

The surrender of official postures of responsibility as we retire and grow old confronts us with the real possibility of stagnation. We can counteract this by becoming our society's collectors of time and preservers of memory. We must maintain our conviction of completeness. Length of life is not sufficient; quality must accompany it. To attain that quality, we must strip away the emotional clutter of the past and devise strategies to live our best lives—for as long as we can. Our journey is not yet complete; there is more to come, and none of us knows where it will take us or what the weather will be like on our way. Circumstances constantly shift, demanding that we continue to adapt.

In short, old age is just like the rest of life, with all its attendant splendors.

> *Now I lay me down to sleep,*
> *I pray the Lord my soul to keep,*
> *If I should die before I wake,*
> *Freeze me.* COFFEE-MUG APHORISM

AFFIRMATION

I vow to meet the rest of my life with curiosity and daring.

TO THINK AND WRITE ABOUT

Your journal is no substitute for good friendships, nor is it a replacement for the emotional support that others can give, but you may find it helpful when you are experiencing problems in growing old. The young assume that the old no longer feel intensely. How wrong they are! You feel joy just as intensely as ever, and you feel pain, too. The departure or death of loved ones, or an onslaught of disturbing realizations or memories, can bring on psychological pain that is often a mix of feelings. Seek catharsis by writing as much as you can, even your barely formulated thoughts and fears. Make no judgments about yourself or your writing. Expressing your pain in your journal makes sure it is recognized and accepted.

Chapter 18

Facing Our Mortality

The Dance Macabre

We were neighbors for long, but I received more than I could give. Now the day has dawned and the lamp that lit my dark corner is out. A summon has come and I am ready for my journey.

RABINDRANATH TAGORE

All of us will die. In past generations, death walked hand and hand with life. Death in infancy and early childhood was frequent, and rare were the families who didn't lose a member at an early age. Medicine, nutrition, and knowledge have changed the nature of that hand-in-hand walk, to the degree that we often forget that death is always as close to us as our shadows. We have developed a sense that everything not to our liking in life can be improved. We have an amazing faith in science. Consider this: Recently, Carnegie-Mellon researchers have been attempting to perfect a computer program to allow us to download our entire consciousness into a hard-drive disk, so that when our body quits, a computer can just take over.

Someone has taken this idea seriously; those researchers are well funded.

This is the single-minded path of technology over nature. And still, all of us die. Whether or not we will do it with wisdom and dignity is the only question.

As we get old, we are faced with weird juggling games, such as the one of having and needing friendships and knowing we can't depend on those friends to be there in the future. More and more we are surrounded by death.

Saying that death is just a part of life doesn't help. Death has always been distasteful to human beings. Basically, it is inconceivable for us to imagine an actual end of our lives here on earth. Therefore, we fear that end. We don't consider death calmly. Death and dying seem to have dense, esoteric meaning—and a whiff of melancholy, like the scent of autumn bonfires.

> ***My days are in the yellow leaf;***
> ***The flowers and fruits of love are gone . . .***
>
> LORD BYRON

Death is one thing not to our liking that we haven't been able to improve. In fact, dying today is in some ways worse than it was a hundred years ago—more lonely, mechanical, and dehumanized. We've let it become impersonal. The dying person is taken out of her familiar environments and rushed to an emergency room. There she is often treated like someone with no right to an opinion. Someone else makes the decisions. She may want rest, peace, and dignity; instead she gets infusions, transfusions, and tracheotomies. She is lonely amid professionals busily preoccupied with her heart rate, pulse, electrocardiogram, pulmonary functions, secretions, and excretions—but not with her as a human being. Or she is "kept alive" by machines that replace the functions of her vital organs and computers that check her from time to time. A light flashes up at a distant nursing station when she finally does expire—to signal the staff to turn the machines off.

> ***They are not long, the weeping and the laughter,***
> ***Love and desire and hate . . .***
>
> ERNEST DOWSON

When we are about to die, it seems that no one wants to simply sit and hold our hand so that we won't feel so afraid and alone. Instead, everyone wants to challenge our death, fight it, hold it off for however many more hours or days or weeks. They are afraid, too.

Fear is a natural instinct, essential for the protection of life. So-called fearlessness is a product of insanity or fiction. But a physician's anxiety may lead him into vigorous efforts to save our life no matter what the condition. A doctor may be quite aware that this is contrary to our wishes, but his own fear is at work. It is easier for the living to feel they are "doing something useful." But it is harder on the dying.

We have no way of knowing what happens after death. Many of us believe there is an afterlife; more believe that such a belief is just another denial of our mortality. The believers think we're the first part of a two-stage process, where first we're here and then we go to heaven. The nonbelievers point out that we've been "up there" and "down there" and we haven't found heaven or hell. As the argument rages, the only fact we have is that lot of people have died and we don't know whether or not they live in some form afterwards. We don't know any more than we ever did in that regard.

Death—

The undiscovered country, from whose bourne
No traveller returns. SHAKESPEARE

Wisdom tells us that whether or not we anticipate life after death, we should consider what we do know of the process of death. Though we attempt to postpone such a consideration until we are forced to face it, we will only be able to change things if we can try to conceive of our own death. We can achieve peace—our own inner peace—by facing and accepting the reality of our own death and preparing ourselves and our loved ones for it.

This existence of ours is as transient as
autumn clouds
To watch the birth and death of beings is like looking
at the movements of a dance
A lifetime is like a flash of lightning in the sky,
Rushing by like the torrent down a steep
mountain. BUDDHA

The process of death, like any other stage of life, proffers us a challenge: to die well. We should want to do this last thing with dignity, to cap our lives with a gracious ending. In order to do that, we should learn what we can expect.

Tell me how you die and I will tell you who
you are. MEXICAN FOLK ADAGE

Except in cases of sudden death, we almost always know when we are nearing death, whether we are explicitly told or not. If we are told, we prefer to be told in an acceptable manner, by our doctor or perhaps by a clergyman. We *will* come to an awareness of the truth, and we will lose confidence in a doctor who has told us lies or was not willing to help us face the seriousness of our situation.

Our family members may share with us their own feelings of sorrow and uselessness, hopelessness and despair. This adds little to our well-being, however, especially if they waste the short remaining time we have in morbid depression instead of trying to enrich the experience of our last days.

Most of us will first react to the knowledge of our coming death with denial. "No, not me, it can't be true." Denial is usually a temporary defense and will soon be replaced by at least a partial degree of acceptance. Denial comes more easily to those who have used denial regularly during their lives. It may take such forms as visits to faith healers. Or it may take the form of inappropriate cheer, laughter, and reassurances to others that we are completely fine.

Some part of us is, however, always quite aware of our mortality. Defense mechanisms are protective and necessary, but what is meant to protect can just as easily suffocate, so that we end by spending our time immobilized.

But few of us are able to maintain a make-believe in which we are healthy and well until we die. Denial has to give way to a new reaction, and it usually dawns, sooner or later. "Yes, this time it is me, no mistake."

> *It was the rhythm of all living, apparently, and for most people. Happiness, and then pain. Perhaps then happiness again, but now, with it, the awareness of its own mortality.* LAURA Z. HOBSON

Unfortunately, denial is replaced by anger, rage, envy, and resentment. "Why me? Why couldn't it have been someone else?" This stage is difficult to cope with, because the anger is often shot in all directions. Even dignified people become furious. "These doctors are just no good." "The nurses have lied to me." We're resentful that we aren't getting more individual attention, individual care.

We need to voice this anger, to have opportunities to get it out. We are better off trying to do so without hurting others, however. This is a time when assertive behavior is a boon.

The third stage, the stage of bargaining, is helpful to us for a brief period. If we have been unable to face the sad facts in the first period and have been angry at people, even at God, we think we may succeed in making some agreement to postpone the inevitable. "God may be more helpful if I ask nicely." We are like children who first demand and then beg for a favor. We use the same maneuvers. And we cling to the idea that we may be rewarded for good behavior and granted our wish.

Most bargains against death are made with God, and we usually keep them secret. The promises we make in return for our requests are often associated with religious guilt.

> ***Altogether, his conscience pricked him a good deal; and when people's consciences prick them, sometimes they get angry with other people, which is very silly, and only makes matters worse.***
>
> DINAH MULOCK CRAIK

But when we can no longer deny our approaching death, these ploys become ineffective. Our numbness, or stoicism, or anger is replaced with a sense of great loss. This depression works to prepare us for the impending separation; it eases a deeper acceptance. Now, encouragements and reassurances are not meaningful to us. At this point, we can no longer look at the sunny side of anything. It would be absurd not to be sad. We are in the process of losing everything and everybody we love.

We are grateful to those who can sit with us during this depression without constantly telling us not to be sad. Mostly, we will endure it in silence; there won't seem much point in sharing it. We are preparing, and we no longer have much need for words. We appreciate more the touch of a hand, or just a silent companionship. Or we may ask for a prayer, because we are beginning to occupy ourselves with things ahead rather than behind. Too much interference from visitors who try to cheer us up will hinder our emotional preparation rather than enhance it.

> ***Men fear death as children fear to go in the dark; and as that natural fear in children is increased with tales, so is the other.***
>
> FRANCIS BACON

If we have enough time and have worked through the previous stages, we will reach a stage in which we are neither depressed nor angry about our fate. We will have expressed our previous feelings, our envy for the living and the healthy, our anger at those who do not have to face their ends just yet. We will have mourned the impending loss of ourselves as well as the meaningful people and places of our lives, and finally we can contemplate the coming end with a certain degree of quiet expectation. Tired and probably weak, we will need to sleep often for brief intervals. This is not a sleep of avoidance.

This gradual increase of sleep is very similar to that of a newborn child but is an easing out of life rather than an easing into it.

> ***It is a lonely business, waiting to be translated to another sphere.*** IVY COMPTON-BURNETT

This final stage is an easier but not necessarily happy period. In fact, it is almost void of feelings. The struggle is over, and now comes a time for the final rest before the long journey. It is a time in which our families will need more help, understanding, and support than we do. In finding some peace and acceptance, our circle of interest is diminishing. We wish to be left alone, or at least not stirred by news and problems of the outside world. We don't often want visitors, and if they come, they will find us untalkative. We may request a limit on the number of people and the duration of their stay. The television should be turned off. Our communications become ever more nonverbal. We may just make a gesture to invite someone to sit. We may just hold hands and ask others to sit with us in silence—or to listen to the stillness, the drowsy hour, the song of a bird from outside, or to smell newly delivered flowers. Such moments may be the most meaningful communications.

> ***The sweeping up the heart***
> ***And putting love away***
> ***We shall not want to use again***
> ***Until eternity.***
>
> EMILY DICKINSON

This is perhaps the most heartbreaking time for our families, as we slowly detach ourselves. They are still very much alive, leaping at each new day. They may not understand our peace and acceptance, or that we have to separate ourselves. How can we be ready to die and leave them?

Even the most realistic, most accepting of us will leave the possibility open for some cure, for the discovery of some last-minute reprieve. This thread of hope maintains us. We continue to be nourished by it. Throughout our lives, we have needed hope. We view Ponce de León as a tragicomic figure, devoting his life to finding the fountain of youth. But in the corner of every ego is the thought that having to die is a fundamental annoyance. Death, however, is inevitable and our lives are setting like the sun.

Like a fine day that has been cherished, the light of it must set. Emotionally, we may yearn for everlasting life, since death rarely seems that it should apply to "us." After all, death is uncharted and dark. We don't want to peer into it. But the time comes when we must. And then, knowing what to expect from the process of dying can help us finish our lives with dignity.

> *If my soul exists without my body I am convinced all my clothes will be too loose-fitting.*
>
> WOODY ALLEN

AFFIRMATION

I understand that some protective defenses are necessary against the fact of my own death, but I will face reality, act kindly, and confront the inevitable with dignity.

TO THINK AND WRITE ABOUT

Whether or not you are facing your own death, it is helpful to see the design of your life to date. Several famous diarists encourage people to try making a "table of contents" for a pretend autobiography of who you are now. What this constitutes is a sort of list of the "chapters" of your life.

If you don't know how else to proceed, begin with the decades of your life—your twenties, your thirties, and so on. Or use the major changes that have marked your life, such as getting married or having children. You could even use the chapters of this book for ideas on how to divide your "eras."

How you do it isn't as important as the process itself. The point is to try to see the direction and coherence of your life's story, leading up to who you are right now.

If you do this now and again over the course of your life, you will see that much of what seems important at a specific time has to do with your values or goals at that particular time, or at least with your understanding of them. Chapter headings appear and disappear according to your present perspective.

Another possibility is to simply list the major events of your life. Narrow the number of these down to no more than a dozen in order to see which have been the most pivotal.

CONCLUSION
The Pattern of Life

The world is a fine place and worth fighting for.

ERNEST HEMINGWAY

We know life is futile. A man who considers that his life is of very wonderful importance is awfully close to a padded cell. CLARENCE DARROW

Pop quiz: Which of the above is true?
Answer: Both of them. So are these:

You're only here for a short visit. Don't hurry, don't worry. And be sure to stop and smell the flowers along the way. WALTER C. HAGEN

Life is just one damn thing after another.

ELBERT HUBBARD

One cannot collect all the beautiful shells at the beach. ANNE MORROW LINDBERGH

This book was never meant to pose irrefutable and eternal definitions and answers, therefore this chapter represents not an ending but a continuation of our journey. William James, Harvard's most distinguished professor of psychology, wrote six sentences that could have a profound effect on all our lives, six sentences that are the "open sesame" to life's treasure cave:

> *In almost any subject, your passion for the subject will save you. If you care enough for a result, you will most certainly attain it. If you wish to be good, you will be good. If you wish to be rich, you will be rich. If you wish to be learned, you will be learned. Only then you must really wish these things and wish them with exclusiveness and not wish one hundred other incompatible things just as strongly.*

During our time on earth, we mustn't be afraid to live passionately. Our intuition tells us to go ahead, but sometimes our analytical thoughts tell us to be cautious. Obviously, we need analytical thinking in order to live effectively; however, our capacity for analytical thinking can be both a blessing and a curse, especially when we get caught in eddies of negativity and fear.

> *Fear defeats more people than any other one thing in the world.* RALPH WALDO EMERSON

James's answer to the fact of fear was that we should act as if we were brave. He believed that if we would only use all our will to that end, then courage would very likely be our reward.

Nonetheless, at times we lose our positive feelings about life, so naturally we turn to analytic thinking to find out what's wrong. And sometimes, like a hamster on a wheel, our minds go faster and faster without getting anywhere. Life begins to taste like the essence of old rope, perhaps the rope of judgment that too often binds us. The more we think negatively, the worse things get. Such thinking only gets in the way of our having a lovely time.

> ***Life is an end in itself, and the only question as to whether it is worth living is whether you have enough of it.*** OLIVER WENDELL HOLMES, JR.

Life follows certain patterns. It is rather like beach glass. Beach glass was once sand. Humankind collected the sand, added fire, and made it into glass. As a glass object, it was used, then it was discarded and again ended up on the beach, where water makes it sand once more. Many fine thinkers believe that life is such a continuum, a form of immortality in which our human periods are part of the flow of time merged with the flow of universal experience.

> ***A human being is a part of the whole that we call the universe, a part limited in time and space. He experiences himself, his thoughts and feelings, as something separated from the rest, a kind of optical illusion of his consciousness. This illusion is a prison for us . . .***
>
> ALBERT EINSTEIN

We have learned that we must value ourselves and assert ourselves, and sometimes reinvent ourselves. But letting go of ourselves—of our will—is one of the most difficult challenges we face. Moving from the closed fist to the open hand. As we take an open-handed attitude toward life, we can be free of the self-made obstacles that litter our path. So let us let life happen to us. Let us meet it passionately and bravely. Let us merge with its slowly deepening, magnificent hues. Then we, too, may take comfort in knowing that we also are part of the eternal continuum.